About the Editor

WILLIAM G. BOWEN received his A.B. from Denison University and his Ph. D. from Princeton University where he is now associate professor of economics, director of Graduate Studies in the Woodrow Wilson School of Public and International Affairs, and faculty associate in the Industrial Relations Section. Professor Bowen has been in charge of the introductory economics course at Princeton and has taught graduate courses in the economics of labor and economic stability and growth. He has served as a consultant to the President's Council of Economic Advisers and to the President's Science Advisory Committee. Among his books are *The Wage Price Issue* (1960), *Wage Behavior in the Post-war Period* (1960), and *Economic Aspects of Education* (1964).

PROBLEMS OF THE MODERN ECONOMY

Labor and the National Economy

PROBLEMS OF THE MODERN ECONOMY

General Editor: EDMUND S. PHELPS, *Yale University*

Each volume in this series presents prominent positions in the debate of an important issue of economic policy

---

THE BATTLE AGAINST UNEMPLOYMENT

CHANGING PATTERNS IN FOREIGN TRADE AND PAYMENTS

THE GOAL OF ECONOMIC GROWTH

MONOPOLY POWER AND ECONOMIC PERFORMANCE

PRIVATE WANTS AND PUBLIC NEEDS

THE UNITED STATES AND THE DEVELOPING ECONOMIES

LABOR AND THE NATIONAL ECONOMY

INEQUALITY AND POVERTY

Labor and the National Economy

Edited with an introduction by

WILLIAM G. BOWEN

PRINCETON UNIVERSITY

NEW YORK

W · W · NORTON & COMPANY · INC ·

FIRST EDITION

Library of Congress Catalog Card No. 65-12516

Published simultaneously in the Dominion of Canada by George J. McLeod Limited, Toronto

"The Squeeze on the Unions" by A. H. Raskin: from *The Atlantic Monthly,* April 1961.
"Labor Unions and Economic Policy" by Milton Friedman: from "Some Comments on the Significance of Labor Unions for Economic Policy," in *The Impact of the Union,* edited by David McCord Wright (Harcourt, Brace & World, 1951). Copyright by David McCord Wright.
"Labor and Antitrust" by Arthur J. Goldberg: from *I.U.D. Digest* (AFL-CIO), Winter 1958.
"The Economics of Minimum-wage Legislation" by George J. Stigler: from *American Economic Review,* June 1946. Copyright 1946 by the American Economic Association.
"Minimum-wage Legislation: Another View" by Fred H. Blum: from "Marginalism and Economic Policy," *American Economic Review,* September 1947. Copyright 1947 by the American Economic Association.
"Trade-unionism and Distributive Shares" by Clark Kerr: from *American Economic Review,* May 1954. Copyright 1954 by the American Economic Association.
"Restraint and National Wage Policy" by Albert Rees: from *Industrial Relations in the 1960's—Problems and Prospects,* Vol. 1, Part III, conference proceedings of the Labor Relations Council (Wharton School of Finance, University of Pennsylvania), November 1960.
"A Positive Wage Policy" by Walter P. Reuther: from *Report of the President to the Nineteenth United Automobile Workers Constitutional Convention,* March 1964. Copyright 1964 by the United Automobile Workers.
"Do the Government's Guidelines Really Guide?" by R. Heath Larry: from *Personnel,* November–December 1962. Copyright 1962 by the American Management Association.
"Shorter Hours: Tool to Combat Unemployment": from an AFL-CIO publication of the same title, publication no. 129 (Washington, D.C., 1963).
"Can a Case Be Made for Discouraging Overtime?" by T. Aldrich Finegan: from *Challenge,* April 1964, The Magazine of Economic Affairs, a publication of the Institute of Economic Affairs, New York University.

I am indebted to Mrs. Virginia Gebhardt for her great help in preparing this book for publication. Special thanks are also due to my former colleague, T. A. Finegan of Vanderbilt University, for his helpful comments on my essay "Wage Behavior and the Cost-inflation Problem."

PRINTED IN THE UNITED STATES OF AMERICA
FOR THE PUBLISHERS BY THE VAIL-BALLOU PRESS, INC.

1 2 3 4 5 6 7 8 9 0

Contents

Introduction

MORE AND MORE, we are a nation of employees. Compensation of employees now accounts for over 70 percent of national income, and the labor markets in which compensation and working conditions are set constitute an ever more important component of our over-all economic system.

In the last twenty years, laymen, public officials, and professional economists have become increasingly aware of the extent to which the success of our economic system depends on the workings of labor markets. Policymaking groups, such as the President's Council of Economic Advisers, have found themselves devoting considerably more attention to such things as the outcome of wage negotiations in basic industries, the implications of dramatic shifts in the composition of the labor force (white-collar workers, roughly 18 percent of the labor force in 1900, now comprise close to 50 percent), and the effects of minimum-wage laws, overtime provisions, and other labor legislation on the health of the economy. "Labor monopoly," "cost inflation," and "structural unemployment"—these are some of the phrases that are used to describe key policy issues, and no one who reads a daily newspaper needs to be told that they describe an exciting, controversial, and often murky area.

An appreciation of the broad sweep of labor-market developments is necessary for an understanding of the pros and cons of these substantive policy issues. The two essays in Part One are intended to meet this need. In the first essay, A. H. Raskin vividly depicts the problems confronting American unions at mid-century. In his opinion, "labor's strength is on the downgrade . . . and [labor] leaders may soon be presiding over the dismantling of their own empires unless they can find imaginative new approaches to the challenge thrust on them by automation, intensified foreign competition. . . ." According to Raskin, changes in the nature of work and in the composition of the labor force are at the root of many of these problems.

The other essay in Part One examines the major trends in

the labor market in this century—the marked increase of married women in the labor force, the trend toward earlier retirement, and the decline in the importance of manual labor.

Parts Two and Three reflect the diverse ways in which events in the labor market affect issues of general economic policy. The essays in Part Two debate the effects of unionization and other characteristics of contemporary labor markets on the efficiency with which the economy allocates its resources and on the distribution of income. Part Three focuses on the inter-related macroeconomic problems of inflation, unemployment, and hours of work.

EFFICIENCY AND INCOME DISTRIBUTION

Milton Friedman opens Part Two with a lively and controversial article on the effects of unions on relative wages and thus on the allocative efficiency of the economy. He argues that "laymen and economists alike tend . . . to exaggerate greatly the extent to which labor unions affect the structure and level of wage rates." But this is not to say that unions have no effect. Friedman contends that the similarities between labor monopoly and enterprise monopoly should be emphasized and that, from a policy standpoint, "it is highly important to have labor monopoly covered by the Sherman Antitrust Act." In the second article, Arthur J. Goldberg, now an Associate Justice of the Supreme Court, takes the opposite view. Putting unions under federal antitrust laws, he argues, would so weaken them that they would no longer be able to perform their socially desirable functions. He also asserts that, historically, the alternative to unionism has not been "real competition" in the labor market but monopoly power on the side of the employers.

This pair of essays, which debate the economic power of unions, is in the historical "mainstream" of labor-market analysis. Labor unions do constitute a special form of economic organization, and the traditional emphasis in policy discussions on evaluating the economic—as well as the social and political—effects of unionization is easily understood. It is well to remember, however, that only about one fourth of our working population belongs to unions, and that even in the unionized sectors considerations besides union strength—the economic environment, management policies, government legislation, and worker mobility—influence wages and working conditions.

Minimum-wage laws are an important instance of substantive government intervention in labor markets; the economic effects of such legislation are debated by George Stigler and Fred Blum in the next two essays. Although the federal minimum wage has been raised several times since these essays were written (it is now $1.25 an hour), the fundamental issues remain much the same. Indeed, Stigler's charge that minimum-wage legislation is not an effective way to combat poverty is, if anything, more topical now, in the context of current antipoverty programs. Blum answers this charge by emphasizing the specialized objectives of minimum-wage legislation and the importance of appraising its effects in terms of the workings of the imperfect labor and product markets of the real world.

The debate on the minimum-wage law centers, for the most part, on the allocation and welfare of the untrained (and therefore poorly paid) workers. At the other end of the skill spectrum, there has been a great controversy in recent years over the allocation of some of our most highly trained manpower: engineers and scientists. There has been considerable talk of "shortages" and one of the real contributions of Arthur Ross' paper is his clarification of the various meanings that have been attached to this concept. The market for engineers and scientists is heavily influenced (and perhaps dominated) by government-sponsored activities. Ross asks if sufficient consideration has been given to the effects on higher education and on the civilian economy as a whole of the bidding away of the large number of highly trained persons for space research and defense-related activities.

In the last essay in Part Two Clark Kerr considers the effect of trade unionism on the distribution of income. Kerr argues that it is necessary to distinguish among several types of unionism and to take into account political as well as strictly economic effects. He concludes that while some kinds of trade-union activities have brought about a redistribution of income, their impact on income distribution in the United States has been slight.

INFLATION, UNEMPLOYMENT, AND HOURS OF WORK

In recent years, the macroeconomic problems of inflation, unemployment, and growth have received more attention from policymakers than the microeconomic problems of allocation and distribution. To this generalization can be added another: it is now recognized, to a much greater extent than before, that monetary and fiscal policies alone may not suffice to satisfy the national goal of high employment and reasonable price stability; "active" labor-market policies may also be required.

"Cost inflation" is a phrase born of the concern that wage settlements between powerful contending parties—large unions and industries dominated by large firms—were forcing a type of persistent inflation on the country which could not be dealt with successfully by orthodox monetary and fiscal policies. The editor's essay attempts to clarify the conceptual basis of the cost-inflation controversy and to present empirical evidence which can be used to judge the seriousness of the problem. The relationship between the rate of change of wages, the rate of change of productivity, and the level of unemployment is stressed, since this relationship is an important determinant of the compatibility of price stability and high employment. If money wages rise more rapidly than productivity (that is, if unit labor costs rise), the formulators of monetary and fiscal policy are faced with an unpleasant choice: increasing aggregate demand will in all likelihood lead to still greater increases in unit labor costs and additional upward pressure on the price level, while decreasing demand will lead to still more unemployment. In the period 1948–1963 unit labor costs tended to rise even when unemployment was 6 percent or lower. The policy dilemma is real enough. In the editor's view, however, the magnitude of the problem has often been exaggerated.

Many policies for dealing with cost inflation have been suggested. The famous "guideposts for noninflationary wage and price behavior" set forth by the Council of Economic Advisers in the January 1962 Economic Report of the President are reprinted here in full. These guideposts, described in considerable detail, are the criteria which the Council would like to see applied in individual wage and price decisions. To overcome the cost-inflation problem the Council has tried to bring to bear on wage- and price-setters the pressure of public opinion and the power of moral suasion. Lurking in the background is the implicit threat of a more specific form of government intervention if voluntary restraint is not exercised.

The next three essays criticize the Council's guideposts policy from very different directions. Albert Rees asserts that the seriousness of the cost-inflation problem has been greatly exaggerated and that the guideposts are unnecessary. Furthermore, he suggests that guideposts may inhibit the reallocation of resources and redistribution of income, and concludes that the government should stay out of the wage-determination arena. Walter Reuther speaks for many labor leaders when he calls for a more "positive" wage policy which would recognize the contribution rising money wages can make to consumer demand. He also denies that wages have risen too rapidly and points to rising profits as a source of further noninflationary wage gains. On the management side, R. Heath Larry of the United States Steel Corporation explains why he feels that, in practice, the guideposts give little guidance; he also suggests that in some circumstances the guideposts may encourage, rather than discourage, excessive wage increases.

The other horn of the policy dilemma is unemployment. As Chart 2 in Killingsworth's essay indicates, the unemployment rate has stayed above 5 percent since 1957. Charles Killingsworth is one of the most articulate spokesmen for the so-called "structuralist" point of view, which attributes a large share of the excessive unemployment to automation and a widespread mismatch between the kinds of skills now in demand and the kinds of skills possessed by a large part of the labor force. To prove his case, he cites the very high unemployment rates characteristic of groups with little education and the very low unemployment rates of groups with much education. He warns that as aggregate demand increases, we are likely to run into "trained manpower bottlenecks." How can these bottlenecks be relieved? In Killingsworth's view the Council of Economic Advisers puts too much stress on the benefits that will flow from the tax cut (enacted by Congress in 1964) and not enough stress on the need for greater investments in education and training.

The Council was quick to express its disagreement with Killingsworth's position, from the standpoint of both analysis and policy. While agreeing that structural unemployment exists and is a serious problem, the Council's analysis of the incidence of unemployment among special groups (including the unskilled) leads it to conclude that increases in aggregate demand can reduce the over-all level of unemployment to 4 percent with no greater difficulty now than in 1955–1956. It would be a travesty, in the view of the Council, to retrain people for jobs which do not exist because of inadequate demand.

With the persistence of high unemployment, the subject of hours of work has received increased attention. The last three essays in this volume highlight the relevant economic policy issues. The AFL-CIO statement contends that organized labor's campaign for a shorter work-week is motivated by the need to do something about high unemployment. As George Meany says in the introduction to the article, the campaign "includes no horror stories of exploited, exhausted wage-earners dropping beside their machines." Clyde D. Dankert agrees that there is some merit in the share-the-work approach, particularly if the reduction in hours is temporary. But a permanent reduction in hours would, he argues, impose too high an economic cost on society as a whole. Reducing the length of the work-week will reduce the total hours of labor supplied and thus the gross national product.

The Johnson Administration has proposed another type of action involving hours: legislation to increase overtime rates in selected industries in order to encourage employers to hire new workers instead of giving overtime work to the already employed. T. Aldrich Finegan carefully explains why he thinks this plan would be economically unwise. While raising the overtime rate would probably increase the number of men employed, he argues that the total number of man-hours worked would decline and the price level would rise.

W. G. B.

October 1964

Part one The Setting

The Squeeze on the Unions

A. H. RASKIN

A. H. Raskin covered major labor-management developments for The New York Times *for thirty years, and is now a member of the editorial board. In this article from* The Atlantic Monthly *he surveys the problems confronting unions in the 1960s.*

A disquieting feeling of impotence besets many who sit behind lordly desks in the glass and marble headquarters of giant unions. True, they still command huge treasuries; they have a controlling voice in the investment of billions of dollars in pension and welfare funds; their strike calls can plunge vital industries into long periods of idleness; their political machinery can influence the democratic process by persuading hundreds of thousands of workers and their families to register and vote. Yet each day brings compelling reminders that labor's strength is on the downgrade and that, like the colonial powers of Europe, its leaders may soon be presiding over the dismantling of their own empires unless they can find imaginative new approaches to the challenges thrust on them by automation, intensified foreign competition, and a dramatic shift in the composition of the work force.

What may be the wave of the future for all labor already has swept over John L. Lewis' United Mine Workers, the union that set the pattern for unionizing the mass-production industries and for modern collective bargaining and strike technique.

The miners are rich in memories and in money, poor in members. They have $100 million in their treasury and $100 million more in pension and welfare reserves. But the industry in which they operate has become an industry of machines, not of men. Employment in the soft-coal field has gone down from 700,000 to fewer than 200,000 in the four decades since World War I. In hard coal the drop has been even more precipitate, from

180,000 to 13,000.

The union's quadrennial convention in Cincinnati last October was like an assembly of the Grand Army of the Republic, its proceedings full of nostalgic hymns to faded greatness. Lewis, still majestic at eighty, was bathed in veneration even more awesome than that which enveloped him when he led the epic battles against the mine operators, the courts, and the White House.

There was much atavistic fist-shaking at the greedy "interests." The few delegates intrepid enough to suggest that the rank and file ought to have a more assertive voice in the organization's affairs were bluntly informed that what they called democracy was just another name for "labor union inefficiency," a luxury the miners could not afford unless they wanted their implacable enemies in management to restore them to serfdom.

Similar echoes of a bygone militancy reverberated through the ratification of a constitutional ban on membership in the National Association of Manufacturers and the United States Chamber of Commerce. The two employer groups were cast into outer darkness, in league with the Communist party, the Nazi Bund, the Ku Klux Klan, and the IWW; joining any of these was made the basis for expulsion from the miners' union.

All this in an industry in which there has been no strike for ten years and in which the employers cheer the union as the chief instrument of stabilization. Lewis, once the embodiment of class warfare, now sits with the operators as a director of corporations set up to keep King Coal from being pushed off his throne by competitive fuels. He and his successor, Thomas Kennedy, promote the consolidation of coal companies into ever-larger aggregations of capital, foster the maximum use of labor-saving machinery to dig and load coal, and cooperate in the squeezing out of marginal mines as a further contribution to cutting production costs.

THE PRICE OF SURVIVAL

The result of the union's shift from guerilla warfare to hospitality toward all measures that heighten efficiency through improved technology has been to keep the mine price of coal steady through the inflationary surges of the postwar years. In the process, coal's market has been protected against the inroads of oil and natural gas, and the unionists still needed in the mines have achieved the highest wages and broadest welfare benefits of all major industries.

But the human cost of this progress is starkly visible in West Virginia, Pennsylvania, Kentucky, and other coal states, where tens of thousands of miners have been tossed on the slag heap to rot in an idleness that has turned their communities into ghost towns and their families into public charges. These human discards stalk the coal-rich mountainsides, scratching out a meager existence at bootleg mines and snatching up their shotguns to fight off the union they once fought to build.

Against this backdrop of misery, the miners' union could do little but implore the government to move aggressively to revive the stricken areas and ease the hardships suffered by its stranded ex-members. It tightened the eligibility rules governing its own retirement and welfare fund to prevent the mountainous load of poverty from bankrupting it. Husbanding the union's financial resources and swelling them through strategic investments in common stock have become as much a concern for the miners as for corporate treasurers.

The union is now the chief stockholder in Washington's second largest bank and has a big chunk of its own money in a bulging portfolio of securities in big coal companies, utilities, coal-carrying railroads, and other industrial enterprises. An accounting by John Owens, the miners' secretary-treasurer, on how much the union had profited from its dabblings in big business was greeted by the delegates with the same warm approval they used to accord news that the union had emerged triumphant from a make-or-break conflict with the mine operators.

No one mistakes the union's involvement in its moneybags for a sign that it has lost either its heart or its muscle. The unfilled needs of jobless mine families so far exceed the capacities of any private group that it would be foolhardy to seek to set up an emergency relief program under direct union auspices. As for the strikes that once kept the miners popping in and out of the pits, they have been abandoned, not from an inability on the union's part to cut off production but from a knowledge on both sides that a reversion to the old warlike pattern would mean the loss of coal's principal customers, the electric power companies. They are equipped to convert almost instantaneously from coal to oil or natural gas, and they have made it plain that any irregularity in coal deliveries will cause a permanent shift to these rival sources of energy. Confronted with a choice between cooperation and suicide, the industry and the union scrapped their arsenals.

THE MARCH OF TECHNOLOGY

Indications are plentiful that automation is drying up the fields of historic union strength; the organizing slogans of the thirties hold no appeal for the new workers pouring into the labor force; surplus plant capacity makes many managements welcome strikes as a handy valve for draining inventory out of clogged warehouses; most menacing of all, increased employer toughness, the mounting pressure of low-wage imports, and public hostility toward wage increases accompanied by price increases have lowered the ceiling on the contract gains most big unions can hope to deliver.

The march of technology is like a pincer movement in its impact on unions. It eliminates large numbers of blue-collar jobs in manufacturing and transportation, thus chipping away the bedrock of union enrollment. To the extent that new jobs are created, they involve hard-to-organize engineers, technicians, and white-collar workers. That is one side of the nutcracker.

The other is the degree to which automation makes businesses invulnerable to strike harassment. When push buttons and electronic control devices regulate every operation from the receipt of raw materials to the loading of finished goods, a handful of nonunion supervisors and clerks will be able to keep acres of machines producing in the face of a total walkout by unionized factory crews. The Bell telephone system and most major electric utilities already have reached this point of immunity to large-scale disruption of service resulting from strikes. In a few years many other big companies will be so far advanced along the road to mechanized production that they, too, can cease to worry about union strike calls.

Even with existing production methods, our ability to make goods is so much greater than our ability to market them that most major industries can satisfy all the consumer demand of a prosperous year by operating their plants eight or nine months. A work stoppage of three or four months saves the employer the necessity of ordering a forced layoff or a short-work schedule to prevent his products from drowning the market.

The 116-day steel strike of 1959, which took a half million unionists from their jobs, made plain how little financial punishment labor is able to inflict on employers through the exercise of its ultimate weapon. Despite the longest union shutdown in the industry's history, the combined net profit of the leading steel producers, as computed by the First National City Bank of New York, came to $816 million for the year, a rise of 5 percent over their 1958 earnings.

To add to the union's frustrations, the excess of capacity over demand proved so great that the mills found it necessary to black out half their furnaces and furlough tens of thousands of workers within six months after a presidential order under the Taft-Hartley Act had compelled the union members to return to their jobs in the national interest. By the end of 1960 the slackness of market demand had caused a loss of tonnage almost equal to that engendered by the long strike. The industry, which is now able to show a profit when it is operating at as little as one third of capacity, decided to ease its embarrassment over the gulf between what it could make and what it could sell by abolishing the production index that advertised its lag to an unsympathetic world.

THE WORKER'S BEST FRIEND

A complex of new factors has further blunted the effectiveness of strikes. Employers are turning more and more to strike-insurance programs to cushion their strike losses: income-tax carry-back provisions operate as another shield against red ink; so do unemployment insurance merit-rating taxes, which make it cheaper for a business to have workers idle because of a strike than because of a cutback ordered by the company.

Add to this a widespread feeling in management ranks that it is time to "stop letting unions push us around." This translates into a far more rigid employer stance in collective bargaining—a determination to get concessions in increased efficiency for every new union gain. Companies that once fought a rearguard action against union demands now make all the key decisions on how much they will give and how much they will take in exchange.

Many unions have found themselves powerless to buck this "take it or leave it" approach because of the vastly increased sophistication with which employers are conducting most aspects of employee relations. All the techniques of motivational research are poured into multimillion-dollar programs to convince the workers that management is their best friend. The blood-and-guts antagonism to unions of the Tom Girdlers and Ernest T. Weirs in the Little Steel strikes of two decades ago has been replaced by a year-round flow of "Papa knows best" communications, the net effect of which is that unions are perfectly all right if the workers want them, but there is nothing beneficial they can do that management won't do at least as well without their prodding.

By all odds, the most skillful practitioner in this field is General Electric, the nation's biggest electrical manufacturer. The extent of its dominance in collective bargaining was forcefully indicated by the rout of the International Union of Electrical Workers in the three-week strike it conducted last October [1960] in a vain effort to improve a G.E. contract offer.

The union's biggest local, representing workers at the G.E. headquarters plant in Schenectady, quit the walkout in mid-course. Other plants were able to restore varying measures of production. Indeed, it was plain that the union's official order to go back without any modification of the prestrike package was issued just soon enough to prevent a general collapse that would have left the union leaders without any rank and file. The only flaw for the company was the issuance by Mayor Richardson Dilworth of Philadelphia of a public charge that General Electric had been guilty of "political and industrial blackmail" in hinting that it would move to a more congenial environment if the police of the City of Brotherly Love did not act more vigorously to get nonstrikers through the union picket lines. The company insisted that its sole concern was with the maintenance of law and order.

It was not until four months after the union had limped back on the company's terms that the first real crack developed in the image of corporate rectitude in which General Electric had wrapped itself. The company was fined $437,000 and three of its high officials went to jail for participation in an industry-wide price-rigging scheme that cheated government agencies and private utilities in the sale of billions of dollars in heavy electrical equipment.

The paradoxical upshot of all this weakening of labor's mastodons in the mass-production industries is that little unions are calling much more damaging strikes these days than their big brothers. Despite the unabated clamor of the Goldwaters and the Mundts for laws to prevent industry-wide strikes, a strategically placed small union often exercises far more economic leverage than one a hundred times its size. This was illustrated with particular force last January [1961] when a walkout of 664 crewmen on railroad ferries and tugs in New York Harbor generated a picket blockade that cut off service for 100,000 commuters, forced an embargo on export freight, and halted virtually all main-line service on the sprawling New York Central and New Haven rail systems.

At the very time that a covey of top federal, state, and city officials were pooling their energies in a panicky rush to relieve the disruption touched off by this tiny walkout, the Labor Department was releasing a study designed to show that there was no cause for public anxiety over the frequent national work stoppages by 500,000 steelworkers. The irritation that stems from this imbalance between union size and the capacity to hurt an army of innocent bystanders is one that damages labor's popularity.

THE END OF THE WAGE-PRICE SPIRAL

The unions have several other big headaches. One of the worst is the heightened cost-consciousness engendered in industry by the recession, by public and political anxiety over higher prices, and by the prospect of increasingly stiff competition from foreign and domestic rivals. So pressing have all these considerations become that there is solid basis for believing that we are nearing—if we have not already reached—the end of the wage-price spiral in such pivotal industries as steel, automobiles, and electrical manufacturing. The decisive battle on this front was fought, in the opinion of many observers, even before the steelworkers went out on their long strike in 1959.

No industry has been more criticized for the development of a leapfrog relationship between higher wages and higher prices than steel. Until 1959 the regular practice of the major steel producers was to give a bigger-than-average pay hike each year and follow it with an even bigger price hike. The result was that steel prices went up four times as fast as the general price level in the post-war period. The union complained that the companies took three dollars in price increases for every dollar in higher labor costs, but it never allowed its objections on this score to moderate its own pressure for bigger and better contracts.

By the time the steel companies and the union arrived at the bargaining table in 1959, it was clear to both sides that they had reached the end of the road on a wage agreement that would provide the excuse for an automatic jump in prices. President Eisenhower emphasized his determination to crack down on any inflationary settlement. The Senate Anti-Monopoly Committee, under the chairmanship of Estes Kefauver, made it equally plain that it felt steel prices were already too high.

Interestingly enough, the union's own membership manifested almost as much coldness to the idea of a wage increase based on a price increase as did consumers, who would have to pay one without the offsetting effect of the other. "It makes no sense to have the boss put a nickel in wages in your pocket with one hand and take out a dime in prices with the other" was a common sentiment in the steel towns as the contract deadline approached.

It was only when the industry demanded a freer hand in junking established work rules that the union unleashed its old militancy. It resisted so fiercely that the companies were obliged to surrender on the rules issue in the peace pact negotiated with the help of Vice President Nixon, but the cash provisions of the accord gave the union only half a loaf by the bread-and-butter measure of earlier years.

President Kennedy set forth during the campaign his resolve to oppose labor-management settlements made at the expense of the consumer. His economic messages to Congress put even heavier stress on the need for wage-price stability. The realities of foreign competition are as compelling a goad to holding down prices as the political unpopularity of inflation. The greater the disparity between costs here and abroad, the more exposed our markets will be to invasion by a fast-industrializing world and the more temptation there will be for American manufacturers to set up overseas affiliates instead of expanding or modernizing their facilities in this country.

This presents the government, industry, and labor with a joint stake in arresting a situation that threatens more import of goods and more export of jobs to the detriment of the American economy and our influence in the free world. With more than thirteen million additional job seekers expected to enter our already overcrowded labor market in the next ten years and with automation snuffing out work opportunities in many sections of industry, the horizons for dramatic improvements in wages or working conditions are murky.

The administered price system, in which union-enforced wage increases became a handy justification for pushing up prices in bad times as well as good, is breaking down under these new competitive factors. In steel, the industry's abstention from raising prices in the last two years has been based not solely on the fear of White House or congressional reprisals but also on a recognition that aluminum, plastics, prestressed concrete, fiberglass, and other domestic materials have joined foreign steel products in a bid for the markets traditionally ruled by an oligopoly of giant steel companies. With the incentive for price hikes gone, the industry is sure to use its vast reserves of unused capacity as a wall against further union advances of pre-1959 magnitude.

This does not forebode a freezing of wages at present levels. But it does create a strong probability that unions will have to be content with increases geared more or less mathematically to productivity. This means producing more to earn more under contracts that will be fairly predictable before the negotiators get to the bargaining chamber. Such a slide-rule system, with total increases of eight to ten cents an hour each year, will make it more and more difficult to explain to the average worker what economic service he obtains in return for his union dues.

THE DROP IN UNION MEMBERSHIP

Unions already are finding that the slogans which attracted millions of workers in the early years of Franklin D. Roosevelt's New Deal are ill adapted to mass organizing drives on the "new frontier." When the American Federation of Labor and the Congress of Industrial Organizations ended their twenty-year war in 1955, the architects of merger spoke optimistically about doubling union membership in the first ten years. With the decade half gone, the federation is fighting a losing battle to hold the share of the work force with which it started. Only about one worker out of every three in the nonfarm field holds a union card, and the ratio is going down.

Part of the holdback stems from the limitations put on traditional recruiting methods by the Taft-Hartley Act and the newer Landrum-Griffin Act. Part reflects the readiness of workers who reached adulthood after the Great Depression, the sit-down strikes, and the outlawing of private industrial armies to take for granted the higher economic standards and civilized grievance machinery for which earlier unionists gave their blood. The long-standing coldness of white-collar, civil service, and professional employees toward unionization has been heightened by the reaction to labor that came out of the McClellan Committee's three years of concentration on the scabrous side of union-management affairs. The firmness with which the AFL-CIO moved to kick out the Jimmy Hoffas and the Johnny Dios has been obscured by the inability of the sanctions applied by labor or the government to force any real cleanup in the freewheeling Teamsters Union, biggest and strongest of all labor organizations.

Difficulties of such dimensions clearly require a thoroughgoing evaluation by labor of the adequacy of its policies, its leadership, and its functions in the total society. Many large corporations have set up special divisions of forward planning to look into the future and decide what the company ought to do to keep growing. Such planning agencies are almost unknown in organized labor. Walter P. Reuther, the dynamic president of the United Automobile Workers, has done more in this direction than his more earthbound associates in labor's top echelon.

TRAINING ORGANIZERS

However, there is beginning to be a stirring even in the most standpat unions. George Meany, the AFL-CIO president, whose crusading for high ethical standards was principally responsible for the Teamsters' exile, is exploring ways to revive the dormant organizing drive and put new brightness in labor's public image. The federation is contemplating a school for organizers as a means of ensuring a cadre of highly qualified replacements for labor's aging general staff.

Twelve of the twenty-eight members of the federation's ruling executive council are past the social security retirement age of sixty-five, and four others are less than five years from that milestone. It is on these men that the primary responsibility falls for evolving a new sense of mission for the labor movement. Unhappily, a good deal of the enterprise they should be devoting to the task is drained off in endless jurisdictional wars. Unions with a hundred thousand workers unorganized in their industries battle over who should control a dozen already in union ranks. Personal animosities are so virulent that the merged federation has been repeatedly dragged to the edge of collapse by the inability of its aging rulers to live at peace.

Yet in many ways labor's elder statesmen have shown more receptivity to fresh ideas and to concepts of social responsibility than their rank and file. Despite the threat automation has posed to the size of their unions and the security of their treasuries, they have recognized from the start that they could not halt scientific improvement. The arguments have been less over whether to automate than over how to share the fruits of automation most equitably and provide maximum safeguards against too high a toll in layoffs.

In many industries union chiefs have been so diligent in suppressing wildcat strikes and fostering increased efficiency that their members have accused them of becoming too company-minded. On the political front, they have been careful to avoid any scramble for patronage as the price of their election support, and the bulk of their legislative program is aimed at achieving faster economic growth for the welfare of all.

THE UNIONS' LIFE EXPECTANCY

The big question is whether the rather amorphous social goals for which labor is now striving are sufficiently appealing to hold together a movement that has always prided itself on its non-ideological character and its identification with "bringing home the bacon" in the most literal market-basket sense. If democratic values are to survive in this country, a healthy union movement will have to play its important role in giving them meaning. To let it sink into a supine subservience to management, with no real grip on the loyalty or idealism of American workers, would throttle at the source much of our productive energy and reduce our chances of overcoming the challenge of Soviet industrial progress.

A labor movement excessively dependent on government would be equally empty of democratic vitality. No group in our complex society has a monopoly on wisdom. If labor defaults in its role as a balance wheel against too much concentration of power in industry or the state, we shall all be the poorer.

Obviously, the life expectancy of unions will be short if all they can promise their members is a modest dose of more of the same in each new wage contract, plus eternal worry about how long their members' jobs will last. Thus far, most of the answers to automation that have come out of collective bargaining consist of little more than termination-pay allowances and arrangements for retraining the displaced workers if there are any jobs to train them for. Developing more satisfactory answers is too big a task for labor alone. It requires a pooling of the best thinking in all parts of our economy—employers, unions, and government on an across-the-board, as well as an industry-by-industry, basis.

President Eisenhower's Secretary of Labor, James P. Mitchell, made some significant headway toward meeting this need. An even more ambitious effort was undertaken by his successor in the Kennedy cabinet, Arthur J. Goldberg. The extent to which these two men—one a Republican with a background of executive service in management, and the other a Democrat with two decades as a labor lawyer and policy maker—have pursued parallel aims is perhaps the best portent of hope that a fruitful partnership can be established on the production front, the battlefield on which Premier Khrushchev has vowed he will eventually bury us.

PROGRESS WITHOUT STRIKES

Labor's trail blazers in the sixties will not be the leaders who plan the most audacious strikes but those who are most successful in devising formulas for social justice and industrial progress without strikes. The two most powerful men in the AFL-CIO, Meany and Reuther, have long recognized that labor must go forward with the community, not by picking the community's pocket for its own benefit.

Reuther began immediately after V-J Day to enunciate the principle that labor should fight against company moves to make every wage increase an excuse for an even bigger price increase. Meany, when the McClellan Committee began demonstrating how flagrantly some union leaders were violating labor's ethical practices code, was at pains to remind his flock that Gompers was not thinking only of dollars and cents when he made his classic statement that what labor wanted was "more." This was Gompers' testament, as Meany chose to recall it: "I do not value the labor movement only for its ability to give better wages, better clothes, and better homes. Its ultimate goal is to be found in the progressively evolving life possibilities in the life of each man and woman. My inspiration comes in opening opportunities that all alike may be free to live life to the fullest."

It is easy to point to departure from this idyllic credo. Too many unions continue to be arrogant or hypocritical in their attitudes toward industry, the consumer, and their own members. But each year brings indications of an awareness that steady jobs and stable prices are more important than the kind of wage increases that erase both jobs and buying power by pricing goods out of the market. Union-built housing projects are replacing slums in many cities; union hospitals and health centers are supplementing community health facilities; hundreds of youngsters are going to college on union scholarships; labor has become a mainstay in Community Chest fund-raising drives; unions are contributing men and money to the building of free labor organizations in Asia and Africa as a defense against Communist penetration. All these are signs of hope as labor gropes for new footholds in a fast-changing society.

The United States Labor Force

WILLIAM S. PEIRCE AND WILLIAM G. BOWEN

William S. Peirce is a research assistant in the Industrial Relations Section of Princeton University. He prepared this broad survey of labor force trends in collaboration with the editor especially for this volume.

COUNT THE NUMBER of persons "employed" in the United States in a given week; count the number of persons who were "unemployed" in the same week; add the two numbers together and you obtain the size of the "labor force."[1] The Bureau of the Census estimates that in April 1960 almost 70 million Americans were in the labor force—about 66.5 million employed (including those in the armed forces) and 3.5 million unemployed. The rest of the population (the not-in-the-labor-force group) is a potpourri of children, students not holding parttime jobs, housewives, retired persons, persons in institutions, and surviving members of the class once known as "the idle rich."

The labor force is by no means a static group. During the course of a year there are many new entrants: some have just finished school (graduated or "dropped out"); some have seen their last child start school and have decided to keep busy by looking for parttime or fulltime work; others may have been forced to enter or re-enter the labor force because of pressing family financial needs. At the same time others have been leaving the labor force through retirement, illness, death, pregnancy, or discouragement because of inability to find a job. Thus, nearly 84 million people worked or looked for work at some time during 1962, yet the labor force never exceeded 77 million people at any time during that year.

1. To be counted as "employed," a person has to work at least one hour for pay or profit or fifteen hours without pay in a family farm or business; thus housewives are not counted as employed. To be counted as "unemployed," a person must not be "employed" and in addition must look for work during the given week. For further details see any issue of *Employment and Earnings,* U.S. Department of Labor.

The size of the labor force depends both on the size of the population and on the proportion of the population who want to work. In view of the marked increase in the total population, it is certainly not surprising that the labor force in 1960 was larger than in 1900; what is rather remarkable is that the proportion of the population of working age (14 years and older) in the labor force was nearly the same in the two years. Between 1900 and 1960 the working-age population increased from 51.2 million to 126.3 million, and the labor force increased from 28.1 million to 69.9 million. Dividing the labor force by the population gives us the "labor-force participation rate"—54.9 percent in 1900 and 55.3 percent in 1960. Furthermore, as the chart shows, the participation rate has been close to 55 percent during each of the past seven censuses. This constancy has led L. R. Klein and R. F. Kosobud to refer to the participation rate as one of the "great ratios of economics."[2]

The long-run constancy of the participation rate certainly does not mean that the size of the labor force is rigidly fixed at any moment; in the short run, the size of the labor force depends on many things, including the demand for labor. As World War II showed, many additional persons, including the retired and handicapped, can be drawn into the labor force if social pressures and the demand for their services are sufficiently strong. There is also a growing body of evidence indicating that periods of unemployment can retard the growth of the labor force by discouraging some people from continuing to seek work.

AGE-SEX COMPOSITION OF THE LABOR FORCE

Nor does the constancy of the over-all participation rate imply that the composition of the labor force has remained constant. The relative contribution that any age-sex group of the population makes to the labor force depends both on the proportion of the whole population in that group and on the group's labor-force participation rate. Table 1 shows the age-sex composition of the labor force in various census years; the chart shows the participation rates of selected groups. From the chart and table, several interesting conclusions can be drawn:

2. L. R. Klein and R. F. Kosobud, "Some Econometrics of Growth: Great Ratios of Economics," *Quarterly Journal of Economics*, Vol. LXXV, No. 2 (May 1961), p. 198.

1. The simple notion that the labor force is made up of adult males is only about half right. Males aged 25–64 consistently have provided only slightly more than 50 percent of the labor force.

2. Younger males play a considerably less important role in the labor force now than they did in 1900. The chart indicates the rapid decline in participation rates between 1900 and 1940 of male teenagers. This is largely attributable to the increasing proportion of this age group enrolled in school and the corresponding decrease in fulltime jobholding. In recent years the participation rate has increased slightly as parttime work has become more common for students. The decrease in participation of males aged 20–24 (not shown on the chart) came somewhat later than that of the teenagers and has not been as rapid. The effect of these decreases in participation rates can be seen in Table 1, which indicates that males aged 14–24 contributed only 11 percent of the labor force in 1960, compared with 22 percent in 1900.

3. At the other end of the age span, the participation of males 65 years old and over in the labor force has also shown a long-run (but not unbroken) decrease. The very large decrease in participation rates between 1930 and 1940 may reflect a tendency for older men who could not find jobs during the depression to retire rather than continue what many no doubt regarded as a vain quest for work. The manpower demands of World War II undoubtedly kept many men in the labor force beyond their normal retirement, but after 1950 the participation rate resumed its downward trend. Even though the participation rate for older males has decreased, this group's proportion of the total labor force has not declined. The explanation, of course, is that the number of men aged 65 and older has been growing so rapidly that, even though a smaller percentage of them are working, they continue to constitute nearly as large a proportion of the total labor force as formerly.

4. The most striking and significant changes have occurred in the labor-force participation of married women (the term "married women" refers to "married women with husbands present"). The urgent need for additional labor in World War II undoubtedly played some role in breaking down the prejudice against married women working. However, as the chart indicates, the

CHART 1. *Labor-force Participation Rates for Selected Groups, 1900–1960*

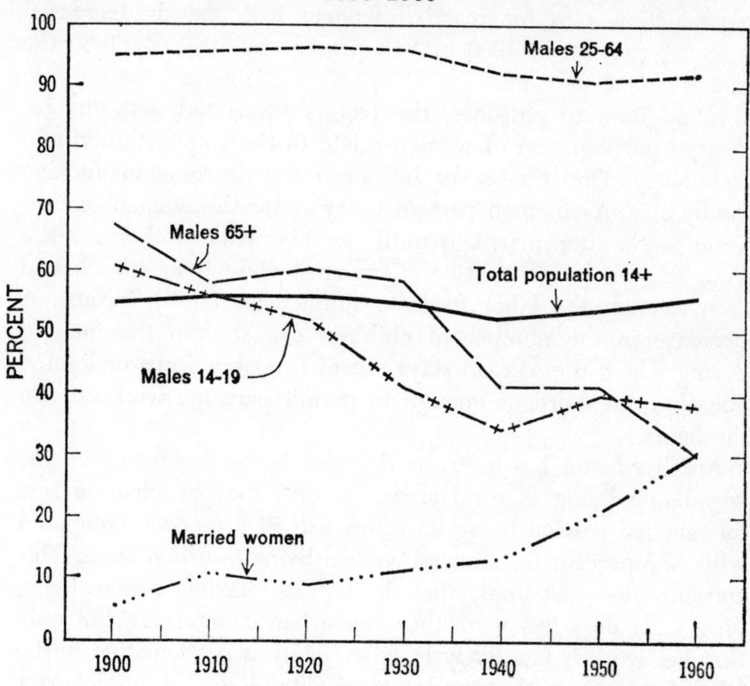

TABLE 1. *The Age-Sex Composition of the United States Labor Force (percent)*

Age-Sex Group	1960	1950	1940	1930	1920	1910	1900
Males 14–19	4	4	5	6	7	9	10
Males 20–24	7	8	9	10	10	12	12
Males 25–64	54	57	58	58	59	57	56
Males 65+	3	4	3	4	4	3	4
All Males	68	73	76	78	80	80	82
Women 14–19	3	2	2	3	4	4	5
Women 20–24	4	4	5	5	4	4	4
Women 25–64	24	20	16	13	12	10	9
Women 65+	1	1	1	1	–	1	–
All Women	32	27	24	22	20	20	18
(All Married Women)	(18)	(13)	(7)	(6)	(5)	(5)	(3)

SOURCES: Clarence D. Long, *The Labor Force Under Changing Income and Employment* (Princeton University Press for the National Bureau of Economic Research, 1958), Tables A-2 and A-6. *U.S. Census of Population 1960*, "U.S. Summary, Detailed Characteristics," Table 194.

participation rate for married women had already increased from 5.6 percent in 1900 to 13.8 percent by 1940. By 1960 the rate was 30.7 percent.

In addition to attitudes, the factors associated with the increased participation of women relate to time, opportunity, and technology. One time-saver has been the decrease in average family size. A common pattern today is for the woman to continue work after marriage until the first child is born; retire from the labor force until the youngest child is in school; and then re-enter the labor force to supplement family income. A decrease in the number of children can shorten the interval during which the woman stays out of the labor force or lighten housekeeping burdens enough to permit parttime work outside the home.

Another factor has been the decrease in the percentage of the population living in rural areas. In 1960 the participation rate for married women living on farms was 21.9 percent, compared with 32.3 percent for married women living in urban areas. This certainly does not imply that the typical married woman living on a farm does less work than her urban counterpart, but only that her work is less likely to be counted as participation in the labor force. From the standpoint of obtaining paid employment the urban woman has two advantages: she is free of many of the chores of a farm household, and she is also more likely to be living in an area where there are offices, shops, and factories, where the opportunity to find a job is greater.

Changing technology has been still more important. Within the home, new products (for example, prepared foods and inexpensive ready-to-wear clothing) have saved vast amounts of time for American women. Tasks formerly carried out in the home are now done in factories, and housewives to an increasing extent have joined the measured labor force. The increase in the number of jobs which are light, clean, and relatively pleasant has no doubt induced many women to enter the labor force rather than remain at home.

THE OCCUPATIONAL COMPOSITION OF THE LABOR FORCE

The same kinds of technical change that have played such a major part in increasing the participation rate of married women have also led to important changes in the occupational composition of the entire labor force.

The "typical worker" in 1900 was either a farmworker or an industrial blue-collar worker. The number of workers in each group was about equal and, as Table 2 shows, about three quarters of the labor force found employment in one of these two occupational categories. Since then the relative importance of jobs requiring heavy manual labor has decreased markedly. Farmworkers, who comprised 37.5 percent of the labor force in 1900, declined in relative importance to about 6 percent of the labor force in 1960. In fact, the absolute number of farmworkers has decreased in each census since 1910. Unskilled laborers comprised 12.5 percent of the labor force in 1900 and nearly as large a proportion in 1930, but since then they have decreased to about 5 percent of the labor force. Blue-collar workers as a whole have just about maintained their share (35–40 percent) of the labor force. This has been due to an increase in the number of (semiskilled) operatives and (skilled) craftsmen sufficient to compensate for the decreasing importance of unskilled labor.

The white-collar occupations have shown by far the greatest growth. This category grew steadily from 17.6 percent of the labor force in 1900 to 42.3 percent in 1960. The jobs in this category vary greatly in pay, educational requirements, and prestige. Included here are not only doctors, lawyers, scientists, teachers, and managers, but also office workers and low paid technicians—not to mention professional athletes. More than half of all employed women are in this broad occupational category.

The other major occupational category, service workers, consists of two groups showing different trends. Private household workers ("domestics") have decreased greatly in relative importance since 1900. During the same period, the proportion of the population engaged in nonhousehold services has nearly tripled. The combined effect of these trends has been an increase in the proportion of service workers, from 9 to 11.8 percent of the population.

No single stereotype characterizes the "typical worker" of 1960. He might be a skilled or semiskilled blue-collar worker, but he is more likely to wear a white collar and work in an office. And the impersonal "he" may very well be a "she"!

TABLE 2. *The Labor Force, by Major Occupation Group, 1900–1960*
(percent)

Major Occupation Group	1960	1950	1940	1930	1920	1910	1900
White-collar workers	**42.3**	**36.6**	**31.1**	**29.4**	**24.9**	**21.3**	**17.6**
Professional, technical, and kindred workers	11.4	8.6	7.5	6.8	5.4	4.7	4.3
Managers, officials, and proprietors, except farm	8.4	8.7	7.3	7.4	6.6	6.6	5.8
Clerical and kindred workers	15.0	12.3	9.6	8.9	8.0	5.3	3.0
Sales workers	7.5	7.0	6.7	6.3	4.9	4.7	4.5
Blue-collar workers	**39.6**	**41.1**	**39.8**	**39.6**	**40.2**	**38.2**	**35.8**
Craftsmen, foremen, and kindred workers	14.3	14.1	12.0	12.8	13.0	11.6	10.5
Operatives and kindred workers	19.9	20.4	18.4	15.8	15.6	14.6	12.8
Laborers, except mine and farm	5.4	6.6	9.4	11.0	11.6	12.0	12.5
Service workers	**11.8**	**10.5**	**11.7**	**9.8**	**7.8**	**9.6**	**9.0**
Private household workers	2.8	2.6	4.7	4.1	3.3	5.0	5.4
Service workers, except private household	9.0	7.9	7.1	5.7	4.5	4.6	3.6
Farm workers	**6.3**	**11.8**	**17.4**	**21.2**	**27.0**	**30.9**	**37.5**
Farmers and farm managers	3.9	7.4	10.4	12.4	15.3	16.5	19.9
Farm laborers and foremen	2.4	4.4	7.0	8.8	11.7	14.4	17.7

SOURCE: *Manpower Report of the President 1963*, Table G-5.

Changes in the occupational composition of the labor force can be traced to two sources. In the first place, the relative number of people employed in various industries changes. In part this results from the uneven pace of labor-saving innovation in various industries. For example, total employment in the motor-vehicles and parts industries decreased about 20 percent between 1955 and 1963, although the number of vehicles produced was nearly the same. In contrast, education shows no sign of using less labor per student. In part, also, the change in the industrial distribution of employment can be traced to changing allocations of the consumer dollar.

Secondly, the occupational structure changes simply because of changes in the "occupational mixes" of given industries. An excavating contractor in 1900, for example, employed mostly unskilled labor. In 1960 he employed skilled operators of heavy equipment and semiskilled truck drivers. In some of the "automated" industries we have been hearing so much about, semiskilled machine tenders and even white-collar workers have been displaced.

For those who want to look ahead, the Bureau of Labor Statistics has prepared projections [3] that, in the main, assume a continuation of the trends noted above. Unfortunately for the makers and users of such projections, however, unforeseen breaks in labor-market trends have a habit of occurring.

3. See *Manpower Report of the President*, March 1964, Appendix E.

PART TWO Efficiency and Income Distribution

Labor Unions and Economic Policy

MILTON FRIEDMAN

Milton Friedman is professor of economics at the University of Chicago. This widely discussed essay was originally published in 1951 in a volume entitled The Impact of the Union.

LABOR UNIONS are important political and economic institutions that significantly affect both public and private actions. This fact raises serious and difficult problems for economic policy. At the same time, laymen and economists alike tend, in my view, to exaggerate greatly the extent to which labor unions affect the structure and level of wage rates. This fact is one of the most serious obstacles to a balanced judgment about appropriate public policies toward unions. . . .

This paper is concerned almost entirely with the long-run effect of unions on the structure and level of wage rates and thereby on the allocation of resources. From this strictly economic point of view, labor unions and enterprise monopolies are conceptually similar if not identical phenomena and have similar effects. In particular, the economic significance of both tends to be exaggerated for much the same reasons, and the fact of exaggeration tends to have much the same implications for policy. In my view, appropriate public policy calls for like treatment of both forms of monopoly—treatment designed to keep their extent and importance to a minimum. . . .

SOME IMPLICATIONS OF ORTHODOX ECONOMIC THEORY

The power of unions, as of any other monopoly, is ultimately limited by the elasticity of the demand curve for the monopolized services. Unions have significant potential power only if this demand curve is fairly inelastic at what would otherwise be the competitive price. Even then, of course, they must also be able to control either the supply of workers or the wage rate employers will offer workers.

Demand for Labor · The theory of joint demand developed by Marshall is in some ways the most useful tool of orthodox economic theory for understanding the circumstances under which the demand curve will be inelastic. It will be recalled that Marshall emphasized that the demand for one of a number of jointly demanded items is the more inelastic, (1) the more essential the given item is in the production of the final product, (2) the more inelastic the demand for the final product, (3) the smaller the fraction of total cost accounted for by the item in question, and (4) the more inelastic the supply of co-operating factors.[1] The most significant of these items for the analysis of unions are the essentiality of the factor and the percentage of total costs accounted for by the factor. Now, a factor is likely to be far more essential in the short run than in the long run. Let a union be organized and let it suddenly raise the wage rate. Employment of the type of labor in question is likely to shrink far less at first than it will over the longer run, when it is possible to make fuller adjustment to the change in wage rate. This adjustment will take the form of substitution of other factors for this one, both directly in the production of each product, and indirectly in consumption as the increased price of the products of unionized labor leads consumers to resort to alternative means of satisfying their wants. This simple point is, at one and the same time, important in understanding how unions can have substantial power and how their power is sharply limited in the course of time.

The importance of the percentage of total cost accounted for by the factor leads one to predict that a union may be expected to be strongest and most potent when it is composed of a class of workers whose wages make up only a small part of the total cost of the product they produce—a condition satisfied, along with essentiality, by highly skilled workers. This is the reason

1. Alfred Marshall, *Principles of Economics* (8th ed.; Macmillan, 1920), pp. 385-386.

why economic theorists have always been inclined to predict that craft unions would tend to be the most potent. This implication of the joint-demand analysis seems to have been confirmed by experience. While industrial unions have by no means been impotent, craft unions have in general been in a stronger economic position and have maintained it for longer periods. . . .

Supply of Labor and Control over Wage Rates · Another line along which orthodox economic analysis has some interesting implications is the role of so-called restrictive practices. It is clear that if a union can reduce the supply of persons available for jobs, it will thereby tend to raise the wage rate. Indeed, this will be the only way of raising the wage rate if the union cannot exercise any direct control over the wage rate itself. For example, in a field like medicine, there is no significant way of exercising direct control over fees charged, or over annual incomes of physicians. The only effective control is over the number of physicians. In consequence, medicine is a clear example of the kind of situation that is usually envisaged in which the wage rate or its equivalent is raised by deliberate control over entry into the occupation.

This line of reasoning has led to the view that, in general, unions may be regarded as exercising control over the wage rate primarily by controlling the supply of workers and that, in consequence, the so-called restrictive practices—high union initiation fees, discriminatory provisions for entrance into unions, seniority rules, etc.—have the economic function of reducing the supply of entrants so as to raise wage rates. This is an erroneous conception of the function of these restrictive practices. They clearly cannot serve this function without a closed or preferential shop, which already implies control over employers derived from sources other than control over entrance into unions. To see the function of these practices and the associated closed shop, let us suppose that the wage rate can be fixed above its competitive level by direct means, for example, by legal enactment of a minimum wage rate. This will necessarily mean that fewer jobs will be available than otherwise and fewer jobs than persons seeking jobs. This excess supply of labor must be disposed of somehow—the jobs must be rationed among the seekers for jobs. And this is the important economic function the so-called restrictive practices play. They are a means of rationing the limited number of jobs among eager applicants. Since the opportunity to work at a wage rate above the competitive level has considerable economic value, it is understandable that the restrictive practices are important and the source of much dispute.

The question remains how the wage rate can be controlled directly by means other than legal enactment of a minimum wage rate. To do this, unions must be able to exercise control over employers—they must be able to prevent existing employers from undercutting the union wage rate, as well as the entry of new employers who would do so. They must somehow be able to force all employers to offer the union wage rate and no less. The devices whereby this is done are numerous and can hardly be fully enumerated here. However, one feature of the various devices whereby wage rates are directly enforced or entry into an occupation limited is essential for our purposes, namely, the extent to which they depend on political assistance. Perhaps the extreme example is again medicine, in which practice of the profession is restricted to those licensed by the state and licensure in turn is in general placed in the hands of the profession itself. State licensure applies in similar fashion to dentists, lawyers, plumbers, beauticians, barbers, morticians, and a host of other occupations too numerous to list. Wherever there is licensure, it is almost invariably in the hands of the existing members of the occupation, who almost as invariably seek to use it to limit entry. Of course, in many cases, these techniques are largely ineffective, either because it is not feasible to restrict drastically the number of licenses granted, or because it is possible to evade the licensure provisions. But they do exemplify how political power can be used to control entry directly. Only slightly removed from this kind of licensure provision and in many ways far more effective is local political support through building codes, health regulations, health ordinances, and the like, all of which serve numerous craft unions as a means of preventing nonunion workers from engaging in their fields through substitution or elimination of materials or techniques, and of preventing potential employers from undercutting the union wage rate. It is no accident that strong unions are found in railways, along with federal regulation. Again, union actions involving actual or potential physical violence or coercion, such as mass picketing and the like, could hardly take place were it not for the unspoken acquiescence of the authorities. Thus, whether directly in the form of specific laws giving power to union groups or indirectly in the form of the atmosphere and attitude of law enforcement, direct control over union wage rates is closely connected to the degree of political assistance unions can command.

Here again, there is a very close parallel between labor unions on the one hand and industrial monopolies on the other. In both cases, widespread monopolies are likely to be temporary and susceptible of dissolution unless they can call to their aid the political power of the state.

THE SIGNIFICANCE OF UNION-MADE ALTERATIONS IN THE STRUCTURE OF WAGE RATES

It would take a major research project—and, incidentally, one that is very much needed—to get a reasonably precise quantitative estimate of the extent to which unions have changed the structure of wage rates. Fortunately, no such precise estimate is required for our purposes. All that is needed is some indication of the order of magnitude of the effect, and this can be obtained fairly readily.

Total union membership is currently about 16 million, or something over one-quarter of the labor force. On the basis of our preceding analysis, however, it seems likely that many if not most members are in unions that have had only a negligible effect on wage rates. In the long view, it seems likely that unions have made wage rates significantly different from what they otherwise would have been, primarily in construction, railroads, printing trades, and in general the areas in which old-line craft unions are strong. Total membership in craft unions is probably not over 6 million, and by no means all these can be supposed to be in unions that have affected wage rates significantly. To this needs to be added persons in organizations like the American Medical Association that are the economic equivalents of unions though not counted formally as such, and members of those industrial unions that have had a significant effect on wage rates. Thus probably not over 10 percent and certainly not over 20 percent of the labor force can be supposed to have had their wages significantly affected by the existence of unions.[2]

2. It is often asserted that nonunion members have had their wages raised because of the "pattern" set by the unions. This may have some validity for workers highly competitive with union workers, but in the main, the

It is very much more difficult to say how much unions have affected wage rates. If the experience in medicine can be taken as representative, even quite strong unions have not in the long run raised relative wage rates by more than about 15 or 20 percent above the levels that would have prevailed without unions; and this would certainly seem like a high estimate of the average effect.

Roughly, then, we might assess the order of magnitude of unions' effect on the structure of wages by saying that perhaps 10 percent of the labor force has had its wages raised by some 15 percent, implying that the remainder of the labor force has had its wage rates reduced by some 1 to 4 percent, the exact amount depending on the relative wages of the two groups. Now this is by no means an unimportant effect; the danger of underrating it should be avoided as much as the danger of exaggerating it. Yet I suspect it will strike most readers as small, relative to their implicit expectations. Perhaps most readers, unpersuaded by what precedes, will regard it as a gross understatement, reflecting simply my own biases and inability to read plain fact. This may be correct, but I urge the reader to withhold final judgment until he has read the section that follows, which seeks to explain why supposedly plain fact may be exceedingly misleading. . . .

WHY THE EFFECT OF UNIONS ON THE STRUCTURE OF WAGES TENDS TO BE EXAGGERATED

If one accepts the crude kind of evidence presented in the preceding section,[3] one is inclined to ask why casual observation

---

assertions are supported by neither economic analysis nor empirical evidence. The observed general similarity of many wage movements in union and nonunion areas is better interpreted as the result of common influences from the side of demand. The presence of unions in some areas merely means that wage changes that would have taken place anyway are made through the medium of the unions. In general, one would expect that any rise in the wage rates of certain classes of workers secured by unions would tend to lower wage rates of other workers because of the increased competition of workers for jobs. But this should not be added to the effects considered in the text, which is concerned with changes in relative wage rates; it is simply the other side of the coin.

3. [The section to which Professor Friedman refers was omitted by the editor because of space limitation. It contained comparisons of rates of change of money wages and prices during three war periods: the Civil War, World War I, and World War II. While stressing inperfections in

leads most observers—even trained ones—to exaggerate the extent to which unions affect the structure of wages. Alternatively, one may seek to determine whether the effect of unions is exaggerated by asking whether there are any reasons why observers should, on balance, exaggerate them. The comments that follow will serve either purpose.

In a dynamic world, economic forces are always arising that tend to change relative wage rates. Shifts in demand for final products, changes in techniques, discovery of new resources, and so on, all produce changes in the demand for and supply of labor of various grades, and hence changes in wage rates. In the absence of unions, these forces will operate more or less directly on wage rates. Given unions, the same forces will be present but they will operate indirectly on wage rates through the mediation of the union. For example, a change in demand that would have led to an increased wage rate in the absence of the union is likely to do so in the presence of the union only through the intervention of the union. Strikes may be required to produce wage rises that would have occurred in the absence of the union. This change in the process whereby the underlying forces work themselves out leads to unions being regarded as causes of changes rather than as intermediaries. In many cases, so to speak, unions are simply thermometers registering the heat rather than furnaces producing the heat. This is particularly obvious during periods of inflationary pressure. It clearly must be significant at other times as well, and a number of examples illustrating this point have already been given.

A second closely related reason for the exaggeration of the significance of unions is that, like monopolies in general, unions are newsworthy. The fact that economic forces work through unions means that these forces work through a limited number of identifiable persons and thereby become capable of generating "personal" news. Moreover, since union-management dealings can only take place at discrete intervals of time and with respect to matters of some moment, forces that would work themselves out slowly, gradually, and unnoticeably accumulate until they come to a head. They must then be dealt with at one point in

the data and the absence of controls for other factors, Friedman interprets the relatively modest differences in the rates of wage increase as consistent with his assessment of the order of magnitude of union impact. *Editor.*]

time and at a stage when the consequences are dramatic and obvious. On the other hand, the forces that bring about wage changes in nonunionized areas operate subtly, impersonally, and continuously, and so tend to go unnoticed.

In the third place, whereas union actions are newsworthy and call attention to themselves, the indirect effects of union actions are not. These indirect effects to some extent reflect the harm unions do in altering the allocation of resources, and to this extent lead to underestimation of the significance of unions. But more important, I believe, are the indirect effects whereby the apparent influence and importance of unions are undermined and the forces which unions bottle up find expression—whereby, that is, the demand for the services of union members is rendered highly elastic. These indirect effects work through devious and subterranean channels and attract little notice. They consist of the somewhat more rapid expansion of an industry here and an industry there, gradual changes in the kinds of workers hired, gradual changes in the consumption patterns of millions of people, the devotion of increased attention to one kind of research rather than another, and so on and on in endless detail. The strike of union typographers in Chicago, for example, attracted great attention, as did the effects of the union in preceding years on typographical wages. The slow but steady development of substitute processes of reproduction, which was undoubtedly stimulated in considerable measure by the existence of the union, attracted little or no attention. Yet this is one of the more dramatic and obvious indirect effects. Moreover, these indirect effects tend to work themselves out slowly, in the long run, and so are difficult to connect with the forces responsible for them.

These brief remarks about the factors tending to exaggerated estimates of the role of unions apply equally to industrial monopolies and serve to explain why the role of industrial monopolies tends likewise to be exaggerated. One striking illustration of both tendencies is that individuals asked to list the most important industries in the United States will practically never list domestic service. Yet the income produced through the hiring of domestic servants is year in and year out considerably larger than that produced in either the automobile industry or coal mining, and the number of employees is much greater than in the two industries combined.[4] The explanation is obvious in light of the comments above. The automobile industry calls attention to itself by the size and importance of its separate firms, by the amount of advertising it engages in, and, in the last few years, by the disputes that arise between the firms and their organized employees. The millions of domestic servants working for their separate individual employers call little or no public attention to themselves.

The bias introduced into our judgment of the effects of unions by this difference in the capacity of unionized and nonunionized sectors to attract attention is dramatized by a war and postwar increase in the compensation of domestic servants of roughly the same order of magnitude as the increase in the compensation of coal miners and much greater than the increase in the compensation of auto workers. Average annual earnings per full-time employee were 2.72 times as large in 1948 as in 1939 for domestic servants; 2.83 for soft-coal workers; and 1.98 for auto workers.[5] Yet, aside from individual grumbling, the rise in the price of domestic service has attracted little attention and has certainly not been attributed to the influence of unions. The comparable or smaller rises in the wage rates of coal miners and auto workers have attracted far more attention and have commonly been attributed almost entirely to union activity.

The abnormally large rise in the wages of domestic servants and coal miners, like the even larger rise in the wages of farm laborers,[6] is, in my view, attributable to essentially the same factors. All three occupations are relatively unattractive; in-

4. See National Income Supplement, *Survey of Current Business*, July, 1947, Tables 13, 24, and 25.

5. National Income Supplement, *Survey of Current Business*, July, 1947, Table 26; and *ibid.*, July, 1949, p. 21. The figures used for domestic servants are for the industry designated, "Services, Private households"; for soft-coal workers, for the industry designated, "Mining, Bituminous and other soft coal"; for auto workers, for the industry designated, "Manufacturing, Automobile and automobile equipment." The ratios for coal miners are not comparable with those in Table 1, because based on average annual earnings, instead of hourly earnings, of a somewhat different group of workers, and because the basic figures come from different sources. The change in the figures used as the basis of the ratios is required in order to have figures comparable to those for domestic servants.

6. The ratio for farm labor comparable to those just cited for the other groups is 3.45. This is based on the sources listed in the preceding footnote for the industry designated, "Agriculture, forestry, and fisheries, Farms."

dividuals leave them gladly when alternative employment opportunities are available—and such opportunities were relatively plentiful during the period in question, so that migration from the respective industries was extremely easy. Substantial increases in wages were therefore required in all three industries to hold even as many workers as were in fact kept attached to them. It therefore seems very likely that the increase in the wages of coal miners would have been of much the same order of magnitude in the absence of the union, which implies that this is also true of the increase in the price of coal. Further support for this view is provided by the World War I experience, when nonunionized coal miners experienced a larger percentage increase in wage rates than unionized coal miners.[7] Yet given the existence of a strong union, the World War II wage increases had to take place through the medium of the union and could be obtained only through strikes, and so the general impression arose that the coal miners' union has been extremely effective in raising wage rates and has succeeded in pushing wage rates well above the level that would otherwise have prevailed.

I do not wish to argue that the United Mine Workers' Union had no effect on the war and postwar rise in wages. I do say that its effect was of the second order of importance; perhaps it was responsible for something like 10 to 30 percentage points of the 183-percent increase in annual earnings from 1939 to 1948. Its more significant effect will probably be in delaying or preventing a decline that underlying economic conditions may tend to bring about, and this may already be in process. . . .

CONCLUSIONS FOR POLICY

The tendency to exaggerate the effect of unions on the structure of wage rates, and similarly of industrial monopolies on the structure of product prices, has a number of possible implications for policy that to some extent are contradictory. The exaggerated importance attached to unions may make it appear that they are dominant long before they really are; or

7. Some of these statements are based on as yet unpublished results of research by Albert Rees to be incorporated in his dissertation, *The Effect of Collective Bargaining on Wage and Price Levels in the Basic Steel and Bituminous Coal Industries, 1945–48.*

that their ultimate dominance is so inevitable that it is hopeless to seek to curb their further development. Evidence that such attitudes can readily develop is provided by the widespread, though in my view mistaken, feeling that industrial monopoly is already so important, and further extension of monopoly so inevitable, that it is hopeless to seek to reverse the alleged trend. This view about industrial monopoly not only is evidence that exaggeration of the economic importance of unions may lead to a similar view about unions, it also directly supports the development of a feeling that the further growth of unions is inevitable since unions are widely believed—whether rightly or wrongly is irrelevant for the present issue—a consequence of, or a desirable offset to, industrial monopoly.

A second possible effect, and in my view a far more salutary one, is that the exaggeration of the importance of labor unions will give rise to movements to limit their power and importance long before they have been able to achieve enough importance to exercise any significant or irreversible influence on the allocation of resources.

A third possible effect, closely linked with the first, is that overestimation of the urgency of the union problem will lead to unnecessary public policies of control and regulation that will push the economy in the direction of centralization of power. An example is the repeated proposal—made sometimes by the right, sometimes by the left—for compulsory arbitration of labor disputes.

The tendency of inflation to strengthen the political and economic importance of unions has obvious implications for policy. It adds yet another potent reason for seeking to counter the widespread inflationary bias that has been developing in our institutions and our attitudes. It increases the urgency of developing and putting into effect stabilization policies that are directed equally at the twin evils of inflation and deflation. At the same time, it calls for no action specifically directed at unions as such.

Finally, if we can curb inflation, the preceding analysis suggests rather optimistic conclusions about the possibility of developing effective policies with respect to labor unions as such. It suggests that these monopolies are likely to be weaker and less widely pervasive than one might assume offhand; that there are important economic forces working subtly and indirectly to limit their power; and that their effectiveness hinges in considerable measure on the degree of political support and assistance that they can command. It follows that it may be possible to keep in check the power of unions to affect the prices of either products or factors without any very drastic measures of a kind that are likely to be inconsistent with our general belief in personal freedom to organize. If, indeed, the current power of unions is in no small measure based upon positive acts of assistance by political authorities, the mere removal of these acts of assistance without the addition of any punitive or repressive measures might prevent any further extension of the influence of unions on the allocation of resources, and perhaps start a slow trend in the opposite direction. Once again the analogy with industrial monopolies is significant. In both cases, we are inclined to exaggerate the importance of monopoly, and to overstate its strength in the absence of direct political encouragement. In both cases, the establishment of a general atmosphere of belief in and respect for competitive forces and elimination of special privileges for special groups would go a long way toward preventing any undesirable economic growth of monopoly power.

It therefore seems to me highly desirable for policy purposes to emphasize the similarity and identity of enterprise and labor monopoly, and the importance of withholding direct political support from either. Thus, I would argue that it is highly important to have labor monopoly covered by the Sherman Antitrust Act, less because I have a clear conception of specific positive acts that could thereby be taken to reduce the power of unions than because such action emphasizes the identity of industrial monopolies and labor unions and the need for like treatment of them.

These optimistic conclusions about the possibility of keeping the power of unions in check do not imply any equally optimistic predictions that we shall do so. The economic power of unions, though exaggerated, is nonetheless already significant and important, and so is their political power. Inflation, however regrettable, seems likely, and with it a substantial further strengthening of the political and economic power of unions. For decades there has been an intellectual flight from the market toward direct state intervention in economic affairs—entirely aside from the influence of the growth of unions in this direction. There are, I believe, signs that this intellectual movement has reached its apex and has been reversed; but this may be no more than wishful thinking, or itself a temporary concomitant of postwar prosperity. In any event, it is as yet no more than a slight break in the clouds.

Labor and Antitrust

ARTHUR J. GOLDBERG

Currently an Associate Justice of the U.S. Supreme Court, Arthur J. Goldberg was general counsel of the Industrial Union Department of the AFL-CIO when this article appeared in the IUD Digest *in the winter of 1958. Before his appointment to the Supreme Court, he served as Secretary of Labor in the Kennedy Administration.*

THE ULTIMATE OBJECTIVE of those who cry out against "labor monopoly" is to put our unions under the federal antitrust laws.

Should this objective ever be accomplished, organized labor will be weakened to a point of almost complete ineffectiveness. National and international unions will be prohibited from bargaining for their members at the plant level and all traces of company-wide negotiating will be eliminated. All this will be done under the guise of monopoly busting.

Employees working for any of the multi-plant employers who dominate the American economy will be restrained from using their collective strength in bettering their wages and working conditions. Instead, workers will be forced to bargain directly with the plant where they are employed as if that plant was a separate entity, completely devoid of the employer's other interests.

For the great majority of organized workers, the enactment of such legislation will mean a return to the nineteenth century when employers with vast holdings held tremendous economic power.

Those who would return to the so-called "good old days" have resurrected the charge of "labor monopoly" as a front for their real goal. If they can convince the American public that labor is a monopoly, then "protecting the public interest" will necessitate placing this "monopoly" under restrictions of anti-trust legislation.

Like the phrase "right to work," "labor monopoly" is now being drummed into the public mind as the first part of this anti-union campaign. Both phrases are equally misleading.

As "right to work" has nothing to do with a worker's right to a job, "labor monopoly" has no connection with our nation's concept of monopolistic practices.

The American public considers "monopoly" a bad word. We say that monopolies are bad—whether created by business organizations or by business organizations in conspiracy with labor organizations. Too often, however, we do not stop to analyze the reasons behind our condemnation of monopolies.

Essentially, our argument with monopoly stems from the fact that competition is economically desirable, and should be the major regulating force in a free-enterprise economy.

We oppose monopolies because we regard it as undesirable for a manufacturer to have complete control over a product, enabling him to raise prices above those prevailing in a truly competitive system. We say that such control enables the manufacturer to gain excessive profits at the expense of the public.

There are, however, areas where we recognize the fact that competition among suppliers is undesirable. For example, we do not object to one supplier of electric power, a single telephone service or a one-ownership urban transportation system. Similarly, our patent laws give inventors protection against their competitors for a limited period of time.

In such areas, we do not ordinarily apply the epithet "monopoly," although in a technical sense monopoly does exist. We do not use the term because in these areas the lack of competition is considered socially desirable.

The same type of thinking must also apply to the charge of "labor monopoly." If a labor union is to be considered an undesirable monopoly, it must be undesirable because it suppresses or destroys competition socially beneficial to our economy.

What type of competition does a labor union destroy? Competition among whom? These are questions that must be answered if the charge of "labor monopoly" is to be considered seriously.

Technically speaking, of course, any labor union is a monopoly in the limited sense that it eliminates competition between employees for the available jobs in a particular plant or industry. By concerted economic action, these workers attempt to increase the wage at which the employer will be able to purchase their labor.

If the monopoly concept is to be applied to unions—under

this false notion—all labor organizations should be forbidden and replaced by periodic auctions at which jobs can be parceled out to those qualified persons willing to supply their labor at the lowest wage.

Unions must be eliminated, under this theory, because the very purpose of labor organizations is to limit the power of an employer to drive down wage rates and enforce substandard working conditions.

If this is not the type of competition envisioned by those who speak the loudest of "labor monopolies," there would seem to be only two other types of competition they seek to encourage. These are: competition between unions to see which will supply labor at the lowest rate; and competition between employers in the sale of their products, based strictly on a difference in labor costs.

Neither of these alternatives will stand the test of careful scrutiny. No one really proposes to establish an economic system under which unions would compete with each other to supply labor at the lowest possible cost.

No responsible social critic believes that competition among manufacturers should be carried on, not on the basis of relative efficiency or ability to produce, but on the manufacturer's ability to obtain the lowest possible labor rates. The social advantage of competition is that it rewards the most efficient producer and thus guarantees the optimum use of our economic resources. There is no social advantage to be gained by allowing manufacturers to compete on the basis of sweatshop wages.

Even harder to rationalize than the question of competition is the placing of human labor in the same category as any other commodity.

There are obvious social reasons for distinguishing between the purchase and sale of commodities and the employment of workers. The owner of a commodity is not selling an object that is part of himself. He is selling property.

If the owner of a commodity is not satisfied with the price he is offered, he can generally withhold its sale until a better price is offered. But the worker is not selling a commodity. He is selling a part of himself—his own skill, strength and energy. The value of his labor, if withheld from the market, is lost and cannot be recovered.

From a practical standpoint, the individual worker cannot withdraw his labor from the market for any length of time. Without a union, he is completely at the mercy of the buyer—his employer. Since the worker must support his family and eat each day, he has no alternative but to accept whatever is offered unless he has the protection afforded by collective bargaining.

Even if the laborer had a withholding power equal to that of his employer he would generally, in the absence of labor organizations, have little knowledge of the market value of his labor.

Prior to the advent of unionism, there never was such a thing as a market value of labor. This was partially attributable to the worker's lack of knowledge of the best available opportunities and also because workers cannot ship themselves to whatever place offers them the highest wage in the way the manufacturers can transport commodities.

In the days before unions, because workers had no bargaining power there was no real competition. There was, rather, a genuine monopoly on the part of employers who could dictate the price at which labor was paid and who were not restricted by market conditions.

Until 1840, labor was considered a commodity comparable with any other product. As such, the courts held that an organization of workers to increase the price of their labor was *per se* a restraint of trade and illegal.

Beginning with the landmark decision of Chief Justice Shaw in the famous Massachusetts case of *Commonwealth* vs. *Hunt* (1842), however, the courts came to realize that the public policy against restraints of trade in commodities did not justify a ruling that the voluntary organization of workingmen was a restraint of trade and a monopoly.

This judicial recognition that the antitrust concepts do not apply in the labor market has been reinforced by repeated legislative action.

Section Six of the Clayton Act—passed in 1914—declares that "the labor of a human being is not a commodity or article of commerce" and that labor unions shall not "be held or construed to be illegal combinations or conspiracies in restraint of trade under the antitrust laws."

The Wagner Act set forth two basic reasons for distinguishing between a combination of businessmen to raise prices and a combination of workers to raise wages. The act declared that the inequality of bargaining power between employers and individual employees depresses wage rates and that low wages are detrimental to the national economy.

This section of the Wagner Act was included without change in the Taft-Hartley Act of 1947 and remains, to this day, as originally enacted.

Congress has long recognized that workers combine into unions for the same reasons that farmers combine into cooperatives. Not only does our government exempt unions and cooperatives from the charge of restraint of trade, but it has encouraged their growth as in the public interest.

Because the worker and the farmer lack effective bargaining power when they stand alone in the market place, Congress has prescribed minimum wages and provided farm price supports. The legislative branch of our government rightfully considers that the national welfare demands safeguards for both workers and farmers against the impact of "pure" competition.

Those who cry out against "labor monopolies" know these facts. They are well aware that the monopoly concept is not applicable to labor unions because unions do not suppress the competition that our society considers desirable.

They also know that in those few cases where unions do cooperate with employers to restrain competition in the sale of commodities, these cases are properly subject to the present antitrust laws.

The truth is that those who make the "labor monopoly" charge are not really concerned with competition or its negative counterpart, monopoly. Their real goal is the weakening of unions and especially those unions which they believe are too strong. . . .

The charge that labor unions are too strong is propaganda. No honest measure of the relative bargaining power of American employers and American unions will show that the strength of the unions is even equal to the strength of the employers.

Whether we measure the strength of unions and employers by their assets or by the results that they have been able to achieve, the comparison must show that there is no truth to the charge of overwhelming labor power.

It is obvious that the assets of even such a union as the United

Steelworkers of America cannot be compared with the assets of a single company like the United States Steel Corporation.

Nor do the results of economic bargains which have been made between American unions and employers support the charge of economic power. No responsible economist can claim that there has been an unjustly high distribution of wages to workers in recent years as against the distribution of profits to industry.

There are, of course, some few instances in which the strength of the union is greater than that of an individual employer. But this is usually countered by the development of employer associations which, incidentally, have not been charged with monopoly although their activities run far beyond collective bargaining.

One of the essentials of our free economic system is that we do not have government interference to redress every individual instance of economic imbalance so long as there is no general pattern of disequilibrium.

The real question behind the "labor-monopoly" charge is whether or not organized labor exercises too great an economic power for the public interest.

The only answer to this question is that America's unions do not have this excessive power. Our nation's industrial scene is not one in which poor, downtrodden, profitless business enterprises have lost every last penny to greedy labor unions.

Wage and profit statistics paint a contrary picture for our economy as a whole. In fact, these statistics show that only a minority of all our nation's wage earners are organized and many of these are organized in unions which cannot begin to match the economic power of their employers.

Even in those particular industries in which the large unions engage in company-wide bargaining, there is no data to support the charge that these unions have equal economic power with their opposite numbers at the bargaining table.

The "labor-monopoly" charge against American unions is false from every viewpoint. The "labor-monopoly" gimmick is no more than a different label on the old box of anti-union tactics still being peddled by the salesmen of reaction.

The Economics of Minimum-wage Legislation

GEORGE J. STIGLER

George J. Stigler, professor of economics at the University of Chicago, first published this provocative article in the American Economic Review *in June 1946.*

THE MINIMUM WAGE provisions of the Fair Labor Standards Act of 1938 have been repealed by inflation. Many voices are now taking up the cry for a higher minimum, say, of 60 to 75 cents per hour.

Economists have not been very outspoken on this type of legislation. It is my fundamental thesis that they can and should be outspoken, and singularly agreed. The popular objective of minimum wage legislation—the elimination of extreme poverty—is not seriously debatable. The important questions are rather (1) Does such legislation diminish poverty? (2) Are there efficient alternatives? The answers are, if I am not mistaken, unusually definite for questions of economic policy. If this is so, these answers should be given.

Some readers will probably know my answers already ("no" and "yes," respectively); it is distressing how often one can guess the answer given to an economic question merely by knowing who asks it. But my personal answers are unimportant; the arguments on which they rest, which are important, will be presented under four heads:

1. Effects of a legal minimum wage on the allocation of resources.
2. Effects on aggregate employment.
3. Effects on family income.
4. Alternative policies to combat poverty.

THE ALLOCATION OF RESOURCES

The effects of minimum wages may in principle differ between industries in which employers do and do not have control over the wage rates they pay for labor of given skill and application. The two possibilities will be discussed in turn.

Competitive Wage Determination · Each worker receives the value of his marginal product under competition. If a minimum wage is effective, it must therefore have one of two effects: first, workers whose services are worth less than the minimum wage are discharged (and thus forced into unregulated fields of employment, or into unemployment or retirement from the labor force); or, second, the productivity of low-efficiency workers is increased.

The former result, discharge of less efficient workers, will be larger the more the value of their services falls short of the legal minimum, the more elastic the demand for the product, and the greater the possibility of substituting other productive services (including efficient labor) for the inefficient workers' services. The discharged workers will, at best, move to unregulated jobs where they will secure lower returns. Unless inefficient workers' productivity rises, therefore, the minimum wage reduces aggregate output, perhaps raises the earnings of those previously a trifle below the minimum, and reduces the earnings of those substantially below the minimum. These are undoubtedly the main allocational effects of a minimum wage in a competitive industry.

The second and offsetting result, the increase of labor productivity, might come about in one of two ways: the laborers may work harder; or the entrepreneurs may use different production techniques. The threat of unemployment may force the inefficient laborers to work harder (the inducement of higher earnings had previously been available, and failed), but this is not very probable. These workers were already driven by the sharp spurs of poverty, and for many the intensity of effort must be increased beyond hope (up to 50 or more percent) to avoid discharge.

The introduction of new techniques by the entrepreneurs is the more common source of increased labor productivity. Here again there are two possibilities.

First, techniques which were previously unprofitable are now rendered profitable by the increased cost of labor. Costs of production rise because of the minimum wage, but they rise by less than they would if other resources could not be substituted for the labor. Employment will fall for two reasons: output falls; and a given output is secured with less labor. Commonly the new techniques require different (and hence superior) labor, so many inefficient workers are discharged. This process is only a spelling-out of the main competitive effect.

Second, entrepreneurs may be shocked out of lethargy to adopt techniques which were previously profitable or to discover new techniques. This "shock" theory is at present lacking in empirical evidence but not in popularity.

There are several reasons for believing that the "shock" theory is particularly inappropriate to the industries paying low wages. . . . A study of [the large manufacturing industry categories which in 1939 paid relatively low wages] suggests two generalizations: (1) the low-wage industries are competitive, and (2) the ratio of wages to total-processing-cost-plus-profit is higher than in high-wage industries. The competitive nature of these industries argues that the entrepreneurs are not easy-going traditionalists: vigorous competition in national markets does not attract or tolerate such men. The relatively high labor costs reveal that inducements to wage-economy are already strong. These considerations both work strongly against the shock theory in low-wage manufacturing industries in 1939. Since these industries were on the whole much less affected by the war than other manufacturing industries, they will probably be present in the post-war list of low-wage industries. The low-wage industries in trade and services display the same characteristics and support the same adverse conclusion with respect to the shock theory.

Employer Wage Determination · If an employer has a significant degree of control over the wage rate he pays for a given quality of labor, a skillfully-set minimum wage may increase his employment and wage rate and, because the wage is brought closer to the value of the marginal product, at the same time increase aggregate output. The effect may be elucidated with the hypothetical data in the table above. If the entrepreneur is left alone, he will set a wage of $20 and employ 50 men; a minimum wage of $24 will increase employment to 70 men.

This arithmetic is quite valid, but it is not very relevant to the question of a national minimum wage. The minimum wage

Hypothetical Data Illustrating Employer Wage Determination

Number of workers	Wage rate	Marginal cost of a worker	Value of the marginal product *
10	$12		$36
20	14	$16	34
30	16	20	32
40	18	24	30
50	20	28	28
60	22	32	26
70	24	36	24

* Or marginal value product, if this is less.

which achieves these desirable ends has several requisites:

1. It must be chosen correctly: too high a wage (over $28 in our example) will decrease employment. The accounting records describe, very imperfectly, existing employment and wages; the optimum minimum wage can be set only if the demand and supply schedules are known over a considerable range. At present there is no tolerably accurate method of deriving these schedules, and one is entitled to doubt that a legislative mandate is all that is necessary to bring forth such a method.
2. The optimum wage varies with occupation (and, within an occupation, with the quality of worker).
3. The optimum wage varies among firms (and plants).
4. The optimum wage varies, often rapidly, through time.

A uniform national minimum wage, infrequently changed, is wholly unsuited to these diversities of conditions.[1]

We may sum up: the legal minimum wage will reduce aggregate output, and it will decrease the earnings of workers who had previously been receiving materially less than the minimum.

AGGREGATE EMPLOYMENT

Although no precise estimate of the effects of a minimum wage upon aggregate employment is possible, we may nevertheless form some notion of the direction of these effects. The higher the minimum wage, the greater will be the number of covered

1. One can go much farther: even administratively established minima, varying with firm and time, would be impossibly difficult to devise and revise, and their effects on private investment would be extremely adverse.

workers who are discharged. The current proposals would probably affect a twentieth to a tenth of all covered workers, so possibly several hundred thousand workers would be discharged. Whatever the number (which no one knows), the direct unemployment is substantial and certain; and it fairly establishes the presumption that the net effects of the minimum wage on aggregate employment are adverse.

This presumption is strengthened by the existing state of aggregate money demand. There is no prospective inadequacy of money demand in the next year or two—indeed, the danger is that it is excessive. If the minimum wage were to increase the relative share of wage-earners and, hence, the propensity to consume—which requires the uncertain assumption that the demand for inefficient labor is inelastic—the increment of consumer demand will be unnecessary, and perhaps unwelcome. (Conversely, the direct unemployment resulting from the wage law would diminish faster in a period of high employment.)

It is sufficient for the present argument that no large increase in employment will be induced by the legislation. Actually, there is a presumption that a minimum wage will have adverse effects upon aggregate employment.

WAGE RATES AND FAMILY INCOME

The manipulation of individual prices is neither an efficient nor an equitable device for changing the distribution of personal income. This is a well-known dictum that has received much documentation in analyses of our agricultural programs. The relevance of the dictum to minimum wage legislation is easily demonstrated.

One cannot expect a close relationship between the level of hourly wage rates and the amount of family income. Yet family income and needs are the fundamental factors in the problem of poverty. The major sources of discrepancy may be catalogued.

First, the hourly rates are effective only for those who receive them, and it was shown in Section 1 that the least productive workers are forced into uncovered occupations or into unemployment.

Second, hourly earnings and annual earnings are not closely related. The seasonality of the industry, the extent of overtime, the amount of absenteeism, and the shift of workers among industries, are obvious examples of factors which reduce the correlation between hourly earnings and annual earnings.

Third, family earnings are the sum of earnings of all workers in the family, and the dispersion of number of workers is considerable. . . .

Fourth, although wages are, of course, the chief component of the income of low-wage families, they are by no means the only component. . . .

All of these steps lead us only to family income; the leap must still be made to family needs. It is argued in the next section that family composition is the best criterion of need, and whether this be accepted or not, it is clearly an important criterion.

The connection between hourly wages and the standard of living of the family is thus remote and fuzzy. Unless the minimum wage varies with the amount of employment, number of earners, non-wage income, family size, and many other factors, it will be an inept device for combatting poverty even for those who succeed in retaining employment. And if the minimum wage varies with all of these factors, it will be an insane device.

THE PROBLEM OF POVERTY

Minimum wage legislation commonly has two stated objectives: the reduction of employer control of wages and the abolition of poverty. The former and much lesser purpose may better be achieved by removing the condition of labor immobility which gives rise to employer control. Labor immobility would be reduced substantially by public provision of comprehensive information on employment conditions in various areas and industries. The immobility would be further reduced by supplying vocational training and loans to cover moving costs. But employer wage control is not the important problem; let us turn to the elimination of poverty.

Incomes of the poor cannot be increased without impairing incentives. Skillful policies will, for a given increase in the incomes of the poor, impair incentives less than clumsy policies. But the more completely poverty is eliminated, given the level of intelligence with which this is done, the greater will be the impairment of incentives. This is a price we must pay, just as impairment of incentives is a price we have willingly paid to reduce the inequality of income by progressive income and estate taxes. Society must determine, through its legislators, what minimum income (or addition to income) should be guaranteed to each family. We shall assume that this difficult decision has been made.

One principle is fundamental in the amelioration of poverty: those who are equally in need should be helped equally. If this principle is to be achieved, there must be an objective criterion of need; equality can never be achieved when many cases are judged (by many people) "on their merits." We are driven almost inexorably to family size and composition as this criterion of need. It is obviously imperfect; the sickly require more medical care than the healthy.[2] But it is vastly easier to accord special treatment to certain families for a few items like medical care than to accord special treatment to every family for the sum of all items of expenditure.

It is a corollary of this position that assistance should not be based upon occupation. The poor farmer, the poor shopkeeper, and the poor miner are on an equal footing. There may be administrative justification (although I doubt it) for treating the farmer separately from the urban dweller, but there is no defense in equity for helping the one and neglecting the other. To render the assistance by manipulating prices is in any case objectionable: we help the rich farmer more than the poor, and give widely differing amounts of help to the poor farmer from year to year.

The principle of equity thus involves the granting of assistance to the poor with regard to their need (measured by family composition) but without regard to their occupation. There is a possible choice between grants in kind and in money. The latter commends itself strongly: it gives full play to the enormous variety of tastes and it is administratively much simpler. Yet it raises a problem which will be noticed shortly.

Even if these general observations be accepted, the structure

2. One could argue that rural families should receive less help, to offset the lower prices at which food and housing are procured. The group is of sufficient size and perhaps sufficiently identifiable to justify separate treatment. But there are grounds other than political expediency for rejecting this proposal.

of administration is of grave importance, and I do not pretend to have explored this field. There is great attractiveness in the proposal that we extend the personal income tax to the lowest income brackets with negative rates in these brackets. Such a scheme could achieve equality of treatment with what appears to be a (large) minimum of administrative machinery. If the negative rates are appropriately graduated, we may still retain some measure of incentive for a family to increase its income. We should no doubt encounter many perplexing difficulties in carrying out this plan, but they are problems which could not be avoided, even though they might be ignored, by a less direct attack on poverty.

One final point: We seek to abolish poverty in good part because it leads to undernourishment. In this connection, dietary appraisals show that in any income class, no matter how low, a portion of the families secure adequate diets, and in any income class, as high as the studies go, a portion do not. The proportion of ill-fed, to be sure, declines substantially as income rises, but it does not disappear. We cannot possibly afford to abolish malnutrition, or mal-housing, or mal-education, only by increasing incomes.

Either of two inferences may be drawn. The program of increasing income must be supplemented by a program of education—in diet, in housing, in education! Or the assistance to the poor should be given in kind, expertly chosen. The latter approach is administratively very complex, but quicker and in direct expenditure vastly more economical. These factors affect our choice, but a thought should be given also to the two societies to which they lead.

Minimum-wage Legislation: Another View

FRED H. BLUM

In this essay Fred H. Blum replies to Professor Stigler's criticisms of minimum-wage legislation.

PROFESSOR STIGLER'S DISCUSSION "The Economics of Minimum-wage Legislation" is not intended to be an exercise in pure economics but an answer to the "many voices [who] are now taking up the cry for a higher minimum, say of 60 to 75 cents per hour."

Professor Stigler's criticism of the proposed increase of minimum wage rates of 40 to 65 cents per hour is expressed in two propositions: (1) that statutory minimum wages are an inadequate means of eliminating poverty—which he considers the main objective of minimum wage legislation and of eliminating employer's control over wages—which he considers to be its secondary aim, and (2) that there are alternative means better suited to achieve these objectives.

Professor Stigler gives the following reasons for the inadequacy of minimum wages to eliminate poverty: (1) because the connection between hourly wages and the standard of living . . . is "remote and fuzzy" and (2) because minimum wage legislation will lead to a decline in employment.

It is true that the hourly rate is not the only factor influencing the standard of living. But the wage rate and the volume of employment are the two most important elements determining the worker's income. A criticism of minimum wage legislation for putting a floor under the hourly and not the annual income is therefore not valid. Such a criticism is based, furthermore, on a wrong conception of the real objectives of minimum wage legislation.

This writer is not aware of anyone who had advocated minimum wages as a means of eliminating poverty as such. It seems more appropriate to state that the objectives of the minimum wage legislation are (1) to eliminate that part of poverty which is caused by the existence of wage rates which do not allow workers sufficient earnings to have a minimum standard of living *even if employment were continuous*, (2) to eliminate unfair competition based on substandard wage rates, and (3) to increase mass purchasing power. Minimum wage legislation is not intended to be limited to cases in which the employer has control over wages.[1]

Given these objectives, the real issue is whether minimum wages can contribute to the elimination of poverty in the way the Fair Labor Standards Act (FLSA) has intended. To answer this question we have to examine the effect of minimum wages on employment—the second main determinant of the standard of living.

Professor Stigler believes that the increase in hourly wages will detrimentally affect the volume of employment. Minimum wages, according to him, will decrease employment (1) by reduction in output, (2) by discharge of workers whose productivity cannot be increased, and (3) by technological improvements which reduce the labor requirements per unit of output. The net result will be a decrease in the earnings of workers who had "previously been receiving materially less than the minimum" and "perhaps a rise" of the earnings of those "previously a trifle below the minimum."

The experience which resulted from the FLSA showed that minimum wages did not increase costs to such an extent as to affect the demand for commodities. Case studies in which the impact of minimum wages could be isolated from other factors affecting production, employment, and earnings have shown that employment did not decrease because of changes in demand and output. But it had a tendency to decrease because of technological improvements. In spite of this tendency, earnings of workers previously receiving less than the minimum wage increased substantially, and earnings of those previously above the minimum wage increased also, though to a smaller extent.

1. The need for minimum wage legislation often exists in cases in which employers have no control over wages. There were few monopsonistic employers in the city of New York but there were widespread labor conditions detrimental to the maintenance of a minimum standard of living. These conditions caused unfair competition in the very cases in which competition was unimpeded.

This seems to show that Professor Stigler's conclusions in regard to earnings and output are incorrect, but that his conclusions in regard to the employment effects are partially right. In determining to what extent they are correct, we must distinguish clearly between the displacement of labor due to increased productivity and the displacement resulting from the inability of the worker to increase his productivity up to the point where it would be equal to the value of his marginal product. It is one thing to point out that minimum wages increase productivity; it is another to criticize the effectiveness of minimum wages to contribute to an elimination of poverty because they lead to dismissal of workers with substandard productivity.

In so far as Professor Stigler has the latter phenomenon in mind, he is wrong. The experience of the FLSA has shown that the productivity of submarginal workers has increased.[2] It is true that there were some handicapped workers whose productivity could not be increased. They were not dismissed but certified as handicapped. In so far as Professor Stigler thinks in terms of technological unemployment his reasoning is correct but meaningless. His criticism of minimum wages for having a tendency to reduce labor requirements per unit of output is tantamount to a criticism of minimum wage legislation for contributing to economic progress, an increased standard of living, and higher income.[3]

The remoteness of Professor Stigler's conclusion from the experience made with the FLSA becomes understandable if we realize that he did not investigate any empirical material. His conclusions are deduced from the following premises: (1) that "each worker receives the value of his marginal product"; (2)

2. Minimum wage legislation led to a general re-examination of labor policies with the objective of increasing efficiency. Improvement of employment techniques followed. Pretraining of employees, vocational schools and attention to lighting were some of the results of minimum wage legislation. See H. M. Douty, "Minimum Wage Regulations in the Seamless Hosiery Industry," *Southern Economic Journal*, October, 1961, esp. p. 147, and John F. Maloney, "Some Effects of the Federal Fair Labor Standards Act upon Southern Industry," *Southern Economic Journal*, July, 1942, pp. 19–20.

3. It is true that the latter results are only potential and do not follow necessarily from increases in productivity if the dynamic forces giving life to our economy are not strong enough to absorb technological unemployment. But this is a problem of a different nature which cannot be solved by stopping technological progress.

that there is perfect competition in a static equilibrium society; (3) that both the product market and the labor market are perfectly competitive.[4] Only when discussing employer's control over wages does Professor Stigler make a concession to the real world.[5] But the main trend of his paper is based on assumptions which are irreconcilable with the objectives of the FLSA and the economic realities within which it operates.

The conclusions at which Professor Stigler arrived on the basis of these assumptions are used to predict that "possibly several hundred thousand workers would be discharged" if the current proposals to amend the FLSA were put into effect.[6] In addition to warning us against mass unemployment, Professor Stigler states that "the increment of consumer demand (resulting from an increase in the relative share of wage earners' income

4. It is true that in his reasoning Professor Stigler fails to distinguish between perfect competition in a classical model of *laissez-faire* theory in which unemployment does not exist and in the real world in which unemployment always exists. But in stipulating equality of wages and marginal product of labor, Professor Stigler must accept the neoclassical assumptions mentioned above. His assumption that wage determination is competitive because "low wage industries are competitive" is only meaningful in the ideal world of *laissez faire*. In the real world a competitive product market often involves labor conditions detrimental to the maintenance of a minimum standard of living.

5. Professor Stigler points out that "in such a case a minimum wage may be beneficial" because the wage is brought closer to the value of the marginal product. This shows that his assumption of equality of wages and the value of the marginal product of labor loses even its theoretical meaning if there is so substantial an element of monopoly as there is in the real world.

6. Empirical evidence shows that this prediction is wrong—even if we accept Professor Stigler's assumptions. In manufacturing, for which we have the best data, 2.3 million workers received less than 65 cents an hour in June, 1945. The overall straight time hourly wage rate would have increased 2 percent (from $0.968 to $0.987) as a result of the proposed increase of the statutory minimum wage from 40 to 65 cents per hour. The additional cost to the wage bill would have corresponded to 3.5 percent of 1944 profits. Mr. Bowles testified to the Senate Committee on Education and Labor that only one industry—the lumber industry—would need price relief as a consequence of the proposed increase in the minimum wage. We may mention in addition that the suggested relative increases in the statutory minimum wage are not greater than those enacted in 1938 when anything but mass unemployment resulted from the enactment of the FLSA. See "Basic Data on Workers in Manufacturing below 65 cents Minimum and Effect of 65 Cents Minimum," Hearings on S. 1349, pp. 1423, 1428, and 1439 ff. It should be pointed out that these estimates take into consideration only the direct effect of an increase in the statutory minimum wage.

due to a minimum wage) will be unnecessary, and perhaps unwelcome."

We shall not discuss the question whether it would be unwelcome to increase the income of families presently earning $800 per year or whether other anti-inflation measures are socially more desirable. But we must point out that Professor Stigler's argument is meaningful only if we assume that large-scale increases in purchasing power result from minimum wage legislation. To postulate such a consequence is completely incompatible with Professor Stigler's dire prediction of mass unemployment.

We have thus far reviewed Professor Stigler's arguments in terms of the efficacy of minimum wages to achieve certain objectives. We have seen that his arguments are largely irrelevant since he ignores the actual objective and the effects of the FLSA as well as the economic realities within which it operates. We have seen, furthermore, that he does not prove his case even in terms of his own interpretation of the objectives of the FLSA. But final judgment as to the validity of Professor Stigler's reasoning is not possible before discussing the alternatives he proposed.

The proposals made by Professor Stigler are twofold: (1) elimination of immobility of labor, (2) "assistance to the poor with regard to their need (measured by family composition) but without regard to their occupation." It is not clear how immobility of labor is compatible with Professor Stigler's assumption. But it undoubtedly exists in the real world and any policy which decreases the immobility of labor is welcome. But it is certain that the measures proposed by Mr. Stigler to eliminate immobility of labor would be inadequate. They could, at best, be a partial substitute for minimum wage legislation—or a valuable complementary measure.

Negative rates for personal income taxes for low-income families are the second alternative proposed by Professor Stigler. This is neither an "efficient" nor an "equitable" means of eliminating poverty because if applied as an alternative rather than as a complementary measure to minimum wage legislation, it would be nothing but a public subsidy for unfair competition and/or monopsonistic exploitation. It would in no way eliminate labor conditions detrimental to the maintenance of a minimum standard of living and would therefore not be a real alternative to minimum wage legislation.

Professor Stigler's advocacy of his alternatives and his rejection of minimum wage legislation as "neither a sufficient nor equitable device for changing the distribution of personal income" brings out an important point. There is at least a presumption that Professor Stigler's concept of equity is different from that implicit in minimum wage legislation. Professor Stigler essentially advocates doles based on the means test. He seeks to abolish poverty "in good part because it leads to undernourishment." And he believes that the "incomes of the poor cannot be raised without impairing incentives." We may remark in passing that there is no explanation why tax rebates would not bring about the same results—nor why they are not inflationary. The main point is that the advocates of statutory minimum wages would probably feel that a democratic society implies a different concept of equity and human dignity and therefore different means of implementation.

This shows that a social scientist who criticizes a specific measure of economic policy should clearly differentiate between the ability of a proposed measure to achieve the desired aim and the desirability of the aim itself. It is true that Professor Stigler says he approves of the elimination of "extreme poverty." But such a statement is far too vague; it is not a clear enough indication of the value judgments in regard to means and ends implicit in his reasoning. In order to make these value judgments explicit a scientist must show the implications of a specific measure of policy, the "price" that we must pay for it, and he must indicate the "price" of alternative policies. This can only be done by taking the existing society as a *frame of reference* and by indicating the *norm* in view of which social criticism is made. It seems that Professor Stigler is taking the world of perfect competition in which wages are equal to the marginal product as a frame of reference as well as a norm for judging the impact of minimum wage legislation. A criticism of minimum wage legislation from this point of view is meaningless. If the world of perfect competition is taken as a concrete frame of reference, minimum wages cease to be a problem and the objectives of minimum wage legislation become unreal. If the world of perfect competition is taken as a norm, the criticism becomes merely formal, devoid of any reality and must lose even the pretense of social significance.

How Do We Use Our Engineers and Scientists?

ARTHUR M. ROSS

Arthur M. Ross, professor of industrial relations at the University of California, Berkeley, has served as an adviser to many government agencies. This essay is taken from a "study paper" he contributed in 1964 to the Report of the Committee on Utilization of Scientific and Engineering Manpower (the Killian Committee).

PERHAPS IT WON'T happen this way, but it could: In 1965 the race to the moon accelerates. America launches a "total effort" to get there first. Some 425,000 engineers and scientists, together with several production workers, are mobilized to telescope the remaining steps of the Apollo program. By dint of this endeavor, the American spacecraft reaches the moon on July 4, 1969, eight full months ahead of the Russian entry. The President announces the good news. Millions of Americans hear his words on their Japanese "Panasonic" television sets, which took over the civilian market in 1966. The people don their "smog-resistant" suits (made in Italy), adjust their "*neue welt*" gas masks (made in Germany), and pour out of their automobiles, in which they have been living since traffic congestion passed the saturation point in 1967. Between the rows of cars they sing and dance in joyous abandon.

Perhaps it won't happen that way, but if it did it would represent the result of a certain allocation of technical manpower. For this is the age of technology. There were times when priests, or soldiers, or lawyers, gave shape to human life. Today it is the scientists and engineers; the rest of us try to adjust and to understand. Hence the importance of allocation, which determines what the scientists and engineers do.

The principal themes of this paper are that the federal government plays a dominant role in the utilization of scientific and engineering manpower; that the results are not fortunate in all respects; that the government must have greater awareness of the consequences of its actions; and that a coherent program relating to the use of this decisive resource is needed.

WHAT IS ALLOCATION?

Manpower allocation may be viewed either as a *process* or as an *end result.* The process of allocation takes place in the labor market; the end result of this process is the distribution or deployment of manpower among alternative uses.

Evaluation of the scientific and engineering labor market, as a technical mechanism for bringing together current supply and current demand, involves questions such as the extent of competition among employers and among employees, the mobility of labor, the rationality with which decisions are made, and the availability of information to those who make the decisions. Certainly it is a competitive labor market. Despite the dominant influence of the federal government in an ultimate sense, proximate manpower demand is exercised through hundreds of employers, none of whom directly hires any large percentage of the total supply. Scientists and engineers have high geographical mobility. They engage in long-term career planning and endeavor to make careful and rational job choices.

The principal defect in the labor market mechanism is the paucity of information concerning this field of employment. Federal and state statistical programs have lagged badly behind changing patterns of economic activity, and university social scientists are still excessivey preoccupied with production workers, hourly wages, trade unions, and other aspects of the more traditional fields of work. Reports and monographs about scientists and engineers are accumulating, it is true, but since the study of the subject is still in its early stages, having begun on any scale only during the past decade, relatively little "hard" information has been established. Definitions and classifications are not yet standardized, so that to the query of how many scientists and engineers were working in 1960, several answers over a range of about 20 percent or more can be obtained. It is ironical that the Bureau of Labor Statistics knows much more about the wages of streetcar motormen than about the salaries of research scientists. Excellent information is available concerning quit rates of production workers in the tobacco industry, but next to nothing is known about labor turnover among scientists and engineers.

One of the most serious informational deficiencies is the lack of knowledge concerning future trends in specialized demand within the profession. A young man entering engineering school in 1964 and planning to obtain a master's degree has no reliable way of knowing which of the present engineering fields will still be attractive in 1970, which new specialties will have developed, and similar questions. In view of long training periods, and the "trained incapacity" of specialists in one field to perform the work of another field, a shadowy knowledge of occupational trends is a serious defect in the labor market for scientists and engineers.

All of this clearly indicates that fact-gathering and analysis must be improved as a matter of first importance; that facilities for counseling and guidance of students should be strengthened; and that educational programs should emphasize theoretical understanding so as to improve flexibility and "convertibility" in the course of professional careers.

Shortage of information not only impairs the operation of the labor market but also complicates the task of appraising the distribution of scientists and engineers. Although concern has been expressed regarding the adequacy of research and development in the civilian sector, the information needed to assess this concern is not available.

Eventually we will have better information, but meanwhile we must do what we can with what we have. Using the information presently at our disposal, we must try to assess the distribution of scientific and engineering manpower among its major uses: governmental defense and space programs, civilian research and development in private enterprise, university research and teaching, and other civilian activities in the public sector.

ALLOCATION AND MANPOWER SHORTAGES

Whether a given resource presents a serious problem in allocation depends on the degree of scarcity of the resource. In a tropical rain forest there is no need to worry about the allocation of water because there is enough to go around. Is there a shortage of scientists and engineers? On this point the economists and non-economists have talked so much at cross purposes that a good deal of mutual exasperation has resulted.

The difficulty is that the term "shortage" is used in a number of different senses. It may mean that professional salaries are rising faster than other incomes in order to achieve a running balance between an increasing demand and an inelastic supply. Salary surveys in the field of engineering, conducted by the Bureau of Labor Statistics and the Engineering Manpower Commission, do not indicate a current shortage in this sense. Not enough information is available about salaries of industrial scientists to indicate whether the current increases are greater or less than average. It is known that university salaries have been rising with unusual rapidity in recent years. Thus, if income trends are used as a criterion, there are indications of selective but not generalized shortages.

"Shortage" may refer also to a condition in which many vacancies remain unfilled at current salary levels. To the layman, this is certainly the most common meaning of the term, but, despite the attractiveness of the concept from a common-sense standpoint, it is not easy to apply. There is no comprehensive register of vacancies in scientific and engineering employment; help-wanted advertising sometimes gives a misleading impression of the extent of demand; employers often complain of shortages in a relatively well-balanced labor market. Furthermore, the number of vacancies is not independent of supply conditions. In an activity such as research, somewhat removed from production urgencies, a "vacancy" may not materialize until a satisfactory candidate comes into sight. Even then the employer may be reluctant to offer a salary at which new hirings are being made because he is afraid of unstabilizing the salaries of existing employees who were hired for less. Thus the concept of job vacancies has serious ambiguities. Nevertheless, it is desirable that greater efforts be made to develop job-vacancy statistics and other indicators of labor demand. This was one of the principal recommendations of the late President Kennedy's Committee to Appraise Employment and Unemployment Statistics, and it certainly applies with particular force in the field of scientific and engineering manpower.

If the demand for some type of employee is regularly increasing more rapidly than the supply, and there are time lags in the adjustment of salary levels and hiring decisions, then it is possible to have a chronic shortage in the sense of unfillable vacancies. Kenneth J. Arrow and William M. Capron, writing in 1958, referred to this as a "dynamic shortage." In such a situation, they stated, "the price will increase steadily and indefinitely but always remain behind the price that would clear the market." Arrow and Capron argued that a "dynamic shortage" was then prevailing in the engineer-scientist labor market.[1]

More recent evaluations indicate that selective difficulties are experienced in filling vacancies. . . . The picture conveyed is of a shortage of experienced engineers in those specialties most heavily used in missile and aerospace activities; a shortage of research personnel with advanced degrees, especially Ph.D's; and a balanced labor market in other respects. It it significant that shortages are *not* reported in those occupations and specialties which are concentrated in civilian industry—chemistry and civil engineering, for example.

NASA states that its requirements for scientists and engineers will increase substantially between 1963 and 1970. In the scientific and engineering specialties where the increase will be concentrated, the increase may well be greater than the total new supply. . . .

The third concept of "shortage" is the most difficult to apply quantitatively and, at the same time, is the most significant. The country is short of scientists and engineers if tasks which are essential to national progress and welfare are not being performed for lack of them. It should be emphasized that this definition cannot be applied by examining the condition of the labor market. Essential tasks may be unfulfilled, for lack of effective monetary demand, even though there is enough manpower to go around.

A corresponding concept of allocation may be stated. Scientists and engineers are properly distributed if they make a maximum contribution to the national welfare in their present activities. They are misallocated if national welfare could be increased by a redistribution.

It will be objected that "national welfare" is an elusive, impalpable criterion. Is there no operational test? In theory, the operation of supply and demand in a competitive labor market will distribute workers so as to yield maximum advantage. But this assumes that the relative strength of monetary demand ac-

1. "Dynamic Shortages and Price Rises: The Engineer-Scientist Case," prepared for RAND Corporation, May 7, 1958 (ditto).

curately reflects the relative urgency of alternative uses, and that the reaction threshold is not too high when there are changes in demand. It hardly needs emphasis that the first assumption does not prevail when it comes to employment of scientists and engineers. A large proportion of scientific and engineering activity (when traced back to its original source) is not motivated by profit and loss. Almost two thirds of research and development work is financed by the federal government; over half of all scientists are employed by universities, government agencies, and other non-profit institutions; and the majority of Ph.D's are in the universities. Reliance cannot be placed on market criteria in assessing the use being made of this resource. It may well be true that the distribution of manpower corresponds with the push and pull of market pressures. But it may be equally true that the market pressures are not a reliable indication of national welfare. . . .

The hard fact is that the allocation of technical manpower cannot be appraised in precise quantitative terms. Certainly better information of all kinds concerning scientists and engineer employment is needed, but such information will not in itself supply the answer. It will serve as an aid to informed qualitative judgments but not as a substitute for such judgments.

Some economists have proposed to quantify the problem by assigning "shadow prices" to scientists and engineers. The shadow price would reflect the estimated true social value of an employee's potentially most productive use, as distinguished from the salary he actually receives for the work he actually performs. Suppose, for example, that a scientist earns a salary of $20,000 per year at General Electric but that he might alternatively contribute $100,000 to the social welfare if assigned as a professor at the University of California. In that event he should be "priced" at $100,000 per year for purposes of accounting and planning.

Shadow prices are helpful when a value can be placed on the alternative use. Suppose that the United States lends money to Brazil at one percent per annum, and that the money could otherwise be used to pay off some four percent bonds. In that case the Brazilian loan really costs three percent. But the proposal to assign shadow prices to technical personnel begs the question of how the "real" contribution of the General Electric scientist in a hypothetical professorship can be measured, as compared with the $15,000 the University of California will actually pay him. Despite the popularity of mathematic models in social science, most of the crucial problems of human society are not now reducible to precise quantitative terms.

DEFENSE AND SPACE

Federal funds supplied to the aircraft and missile, and electrical equipment and communication industries accounted for almost half of all research and development work conducted anywhere in private industry, for any purpose and under any sponsorship, during the year 1962.

One would expect an unusually high consumption of research and development manpower in space and defense because the whole emphasis has shifted to advanced development rather than mass production. So rapidly does military technology change that it may be entirely rational never to produce an item after spending billions to develop it. Moreover, this is a situation where the customer does not know in advance exactly what he wants; the supplier does not know in advance what he can really deliver; the serviceability of the product will not be entirely clear until it has been developed and tested. Under these circumstances a good deal of apparent waste motion is inevitable, especially when judged in retrospect. I can only state my impressions based on what I have seen, heard, and read. Nevertheless, there is a good deal of evidence pointing in the direction of prodigality, indicating that while the federal agencies have been operating under budgetary constraints, first-rate manpower has been pre-empted by contractors as if the supply were unlimited. These indications give rise to a number of important issues.

1. *Large number of weapons systems developed at great cost but never put into production.*
2. *Large number of companies competing for research and development or production contracts in special fields such as orbital-guidance equipment.* Each company must have its own staff of scientists and engineers. While competition is desirable, has not a great deal of overcapacity been generated? . . .

3. *Consumption of scientific and engineering manpower in preparing and selling proposals.* If it is true that 5 to 10 percent of all research and development personnel in defense industries are occupied in this fashion, there is justification for suspecting that wasteful competition has been stimulated.
4. *Assignment of scientists and engineers to sub-professional and administrative duties. . . .*
5. *Manpower "loading" or "hoarding" in order to be in a position to accept new contracts. . . .*
6. *Lack of pressure on the contractor to minimize cost. . . .*

Thus the factors that encourage wasteful use of scientific and engineering manpower in defense and space activities are much more fundamental than the adequacy of personnel management or the quality of human relations. They are inherent in the system of program determination, contractor selection, contract negotiation, and administration. In my judgment, consumption of scientists and engineers might be significantly reduced without sacrificing the program goals.

CIVILIAN RESEARCH AND DEVELOPMENT IN PRIVATE ENTERPRISE

The growth of research and development in the postwar period was so phenomenal that a progressive intensification has been taken for granted. Professor Machlup of Princeton, author of a treatise on *The Production and Distribution of Knowledge in the United States,* tells us that research and development grew at an annual rate of 19.8 percent between 1940 and 1963.[2]

Federal expenditures related to defense and space purposes account for much of the increase. The build-up of company-financed research and development (primarily but not exclusively related to civilian production) has been less spectacular. Furthermore, the intensification of company-financed research and development seems to have tapered off to a considerable extent after 1957.

Aside from this retardation, there are other sobering facts that cast doubt on ebullient statements concerning the extent to which research and development has penetrated American industry. Only seven industries spent as much as $200,000,000 of

2. Fritz Machlup, *The Production and Distribution of Knowledge in the United States* (Princeton, 1962), pp. 155–156.

Expenditures on R & D in 1962

Chemicals and allied products	$894,000,000
Electrical equipment and communications	887,000,000
Motor vehicles and other transportation equipment	675,000,000
Machinery	633,000,000
Aircraft and missiles	412,000,000
Petroleum refining and extraction	281,000,000
Professional and scientific instruments	231,000,000
Total, seven industries	$4,013,000,000

their own money for research and development in 1962.

Although these industries were responsible for 83 percent of all company-financed research and development, they represented only 10 percent of total employment and 35 percent of manufacturing employment.

At the other end of the spectrum, consider the following six industries: food and kindred products; textiles and apparel; lumber, wood products and furniture; paper and allied products; primary metals; and fabricated metal products. These industries are much larger than the other seven, accounting for 14 percent of total employment and 49 percent of manufacturing employment. However, in 1960 they spent only $424,000,000 of their own funds for research and development, less than 10 percent of the total.

It should be added that very little research and development work is conducted in non-manufacturing industries, where the bulk of the gross national product is produced; and that 200 firms account for over three fourths of all company-financed research and development.[3]

Thus the status of civilian research and development in the United States is not too reassuring. Most of it is done by large firms in a few manufacturing industries. In relation to total output it has not grown much since 1957.

Persistent complaints are voiced that civilian research and development is being hampered by the shortage of competent engineers and scientists and the rising level of salary costs. But

3. Research and development statistics in the preceding four paragraphs are from National Science Foundation, *Research and Development in Industry 1960* (Washington, 1963). Employment statistics are calculated from Bureau of Labor Statistics data.

the available evidence does not support the explanation for the slowdown. It is true that selective shortages are reported, but these are mainly in the specialties most closely related to space and defense programs. It does not appear that civil engineers, chemical engineers, chemists, geologists, or biologists are in short supply (except for those with advanced degrees).

If there were serious shortages in the labor market, we would expect salary increases to be somewhat higher than average. Available information concerning engineering salaries, however, indicates that recent increases have been below average.

It is sometimes argued that, although engineers as a whole may be in adequate supply, there is a real shortage of the more creative and capable individuals. In a certain sense, there is always a shortage of highly creative individuals in any field. Yet it is significant that, according to government salary surveys, the more highly remunerated groups of engineers (generally in the $15,000–$25,000 class) did not receive higher increases than the other groups.

Additional doubt is cast on claims of an engineer shortage by declining enrollments in engineering schools during recent years. Prospective earnings are not the only consideration, of course, that leads a talented young person with a scientific turn of mind to make his choice among engineering, medicine, physics, chemistry, and other professions utilizing that type of ability. There are also changes in the prestige hierarchy of professionals, differences in the availability of educational facilities, and other related factors. But, by and large, the economic influences continue to operate. If a profession is in great demand, jobs are plentiful, relative earnings rise, and young people are drawn into it.

National Science Foundation statistics on "performance cost" per research and development scientist and engineer (which includes materials, equipment and facilities as well as personnel) show a relatively modest increase, from $33,300 in 1957 to $34,700 in 1961. There have been substantial increases in certain industries, including food and kindred products; textiles and apparel; lumber, wood products, and furniture; and primary metals. These industries never have done a large amount of research and development, however, even when their costs were lower.

My over-all judgment is that the retardation of civilian research and development must be explained by reasons other than manpower shortages.

Probably the principal reason is the slowdown in economic growth. Investment in plants and facilities depends upon the anticipated profitability (or "marginal efficiency") of such investment, together with the cost and availability of funds. There is no indication that industry is short of funds; in fact, the evidence is to the contrary. The prospective reduction in individual and corporate income taxes will probably stimulate private investment. If so, it can be anticipated that civilian research and development will then begin to accelerate once more.

But even when this happens, research and development will still be concentrated in a relatively confined sector of the economy—the larger companies in certain manufacturing industries. Smaller companies—aside from specialized research organizations—typically do not have the resources for this type of work, which is inevitably speculative and must be projected toward a distant time horizon. It follows that in industries (such as furniture and apparel) in which small firms predominate, research and development will have to be done by cooperative associations or by government support if it is to be done on any substantial scale.

The idea of government-supported civilian research and development will inevitably encounter strenuous opposition. Such activity may well undermine the value of existing patents, processes, and capital equipment. There are also objections based on principle, but, in view of the already dominant position of the federal government in agricultural and medical research, the entry of the government into other fields would hardly constitute a precedent. . . .

Trade-unionism and Distributive Shares

CLARK KERR

Clark Kerr, now president of the University of California, has written extensively in the field of industrial relations. This paper was presented at the 60th annual meeting of the American Economic Association and was first published in May 1954.

IT IS A PERENNIAL question whether trade-unionism plays the role of Robin Hood or Jesse James. Robin Hood was the legendary hero of the people, albeit he is now considered a subversive character in some quarters, who robbed the rich to aid the poor and did so in a most sportsmanlike manner. Jesse James was the bad man who robbed the rich and the poor alike with nothing but loss to society.

This question is an interesting and perhaps even urgent one, but to answer it three other questions must first be answered: (1) Can trade-unionism redistribute income? (2) Does it, within a given context, have the actual power and the motivation to do so? (3) What are the consequences if it both can and does? This paper is concerned only with the first of these three questions and with only a part, although a major part, of that question. Specifically it discusses whether trade-unionism can affect the distribution of national income as between wages, or wages and salaries, on the one hand, and profits or entrepreneurial income, rent and interest, on the other. . . .

Now the term "trade-unionism" instead of "collective bargaining" is used deliberately. Unions can and do affect actions of both employers and governments, and some of both kinds of actions have potential or actual consequences for distributive shares. To explore the impact of unionism in only the economic and not also the political sphere is to tell but half the tale.

Any approach to this problem encounters two important obstacles. The first is the great lack of adequate statistics covering long enough time periods for a sufficient number of countries so that definitive conclusions might be reached. The second is even more formidable. It is that so much more is changing in a dynamic economy than just the amount and the direction of the power of trade-unions. To separate out this single factor alone, with any great degree of precision, is impossible.

Consequently, we must, as yet, rely on judgment rather than rigorous analysis, and the judgment of the economists who have commented on the question of whether trade-unionism can affect distributive shares has varied.

The confusion of tongues may come, in part, from the apparent simplicity of the question as customarily phrased: Does (or can) trade-unionism (or collective bargaining) affect distributive shares? An affirmative or negative answer seems required. A more fruitful phrasing of the question might be: Under what circumstances, if any, will trade-unionism affect distributive shares and in what fashion? Trade-unionism is more than one thing and it operates in more than a single environment. It is the thesis of this paper that a certain kind of trade-unionism under certain conditions will have no effect; that a certain kind of trade-unionism under certain conditions will raise labor's share; and that a certain kind of trade-unionism under certain conditions will reduce labor's share.

First, we shall present several kinds of trade-unionism; second, the results they are likely to have in the environment or environments appropriate to each; and, third, the American and British experiences in relationship to this analysis.

SIX TYPES OF UNIONISM

Unionism may be categorized in many ways for many purposes. For our purpose it is useful to distinguish among types of unionism in accordance with their broad economic purposes and whether these purposes are implemented through collective bargaining or through political action. We distinguish here among six types of unionism according to their attempted depth of penetration into economic processes and according to their reliance on economic or political methods. Depth of penetration is shown by three levels: bargaining over the money wage, bargaining over the real wage, and bargaining over distributive shares. These three levels of penetration taken together with the two kinds of methods—collective bargaining and political action—

yield us our six types. . . .

The six types of unionism—or, perhaps better, the six programs of unionism—follow:

1. *Pure and simple unionism.* Here the emphasis is on collective bargaining to raise the money wage.

2. *New Deal unionism.* The essence of this type is a political alliance with other forces also concerned with securing a full employment economy through governmental action while bargaining for a higher money wage under the improved economic conditions.

3. *Improvement unionism.* In this type the union bargains with the employer for a real wage (the escalator clause) and a share of increased productivity (the improvement clause). It is unionism which is still pure but no longer so simple. "Pure and simple unionism" will, of course, also react to changes in the price level and in productivity but in a more informal manner.

4. *Direct-controls unionism.* Direct governmental controls on a permanent basis are sought, particularly over prices. This is a counterpart of "improvement unionism" with a national bargain at the parliamentary level taking the place of a plant or industry-wide or even nation-wide bargain across the conference table. In Norway, the unions and the social democratic party have sought and secured a permanent price control law; and unions in the United States and Great Britain have been more favorably disposed to direct controls, under certain conditions, than have most other elements in the population. The Swedish trade-union federation seeks permanent price control on "monopoly products."

5. *Managerial unionism.* Unions adopting this approach try to affect distributive shares at the plant or industry level through such devices as M. Bronfenbrenner has set forth in his article, "Wages in Excess of Marginal Revenue Product" (*Southern Economic Journal,* January, 1950): the "all-or-none" contract, profit-sharing schemes, union-management joint control of the industry with the union participating in price setting, control of entry of firms, and so forth. This might be called "not so pure and not so simple unionism."

6. *Labor party unionism.* Here again the effort is to control distributive shares but through influencing governmental action instead of through collective bargaining, by way of progressive taxation and various forms of subsidies.

PURSUIT AND ESCAPE

Each of these types of unionism is engaged in a grand pursuit—a pursuit mainly of the employer. And the employer is always trying, with more or less success, to escape. Now I do not wish to conjure up a picture of poor Eliza being chased across the ice by bloodhounds. Our Eliza is by no means always poor; nor do the bloodhounds always pursue very aggressively (they are often quite gentle creatures); and, moreover, in our drama Eliza does not always get across the river in time. Beyond that, the bloodhounds sometimes catch somebody else while chasing Eliza. They may even, inadvertently, catch themselves.

It is to this pursuit of the employer by unionism that we now turn our attention. The end conclusion will be that only through quite deep penetration into economic decision-making, either directly or indirectly through government, can unionism raise labor's share more than temporarily; and that unionism must approach the problem of distributive shares directly and consciously if it is to attain the goal of a higher relative share for labor. In the discussion which follows we shall relate type of program to degree of change. This assumes, of course, that unionism has the power to make each program effective. We shall, however, be taking power for granted and concentrating on the program and its likely results; but it should be understood throughout that the results will depend on power as well as on program. . . .

Pure and Simple Unionism · It is relatively easy for employers not to be caught by the economic program of pure and simple unionism. To begin with, union wages may not be raised above the rates which otherwise would have prevailed. If they are, there are two important links between wages and profits, and employers may elude pursuit at either or both of these two points. First, they may raise prices (and this is particularly easy to do if the union covers the whole industry); and, second, they may introduce laborsaving devices or otherwise raise productivity. Thus one would expect this kind of program to result in a higher share for labor only when unionism was particularly aggressive, as perhaps in its organizing period; when the market was "hard," to borrow the phrase of Phelps Brown and Hart, i.e., when it was pressing down on prices; and when labor-saving innovations or other improvements in the use of labor were not available.

Presumably such gains in labor's share at the expense of profits would usually be only temporary, although Phelps Brown and Hart have suggested that employers once having had their margins cut may be content to leave them at lower levels for substantial periods of time and perhaps even permanently.

Pure and simple unionism may, under some circumstances, actually reduce labor's share and raise the share of profits, although by mentioning this possibility I do not wish to imply that it is a very normal occurrence. With the introduction by unionism of what the Webbs called the "standard rate," the natural spread of rates over a wide range from firm to firm is greatly reduced or even eliminated. Within this range, in the absence of unionism, firms are distributed in the wage rates they offer largely in accordance with their ability to pay. The more efficient firms, in effect, share their larger profits informally with their employees. Good behavior by an employer consists of paying in excess of the going rate. Under the standard rate policy, however, it consists of paying the union rate. However, wage supplements, now quite important in many industries, are less likely to be standardized. Given any substantial degree of union sensitivity to the volume of employment, the standard rate will be set well below the capacity to pay of the more efficient firms. Some firms may be forced out of business, although this seldom occurs, and others may have their profit margins reduced, but for others the standard rate preserves for the firm itself that portion of profits it otherwise would have shared with labor. Whether the profit share would be larger more than temporarily, if at all, would, of course, depend on many things, including what happened to the entry of new firms, to prices, and to the volume of employment.

New Deal Unionism · Under a program emphasizing the achievement of full employment through governmental policy, unions can chase employers faster with higher money wages than in periods marked by less than full employment, but employers can run still faster. The profit share rises and, even though the shares for rent and interest are reduced, labor's relative share of national income falls. In a depression, exactly the reverse happens and labor's share rises. Within this share, the salary share rises more than the wage share, but the wage share also increases.

Thus, over a period of time, a permanent full employment economy will show a lower average share for labor than one where prosperity and depression alternate. The permanent full employment economy, however, may show a higher share for labor than the prosperity period of a less stable economy, particularly because continued full employment and the conditions associated with it bring a shift away from debt and a reduction in interest rates. (The share of rent, however, may rise over time because rents themselves, however sluggish, will tend to rise.) An economy with continuing full employment without inflation may also show a higher share for labor than one rapidly approaching full employment because wages will not be lagging behind prices as they do in this latter case. However, if permanent full employment is accompanied by constant inflation, lags will tend to hold the wage share down and the profit share up. Consequently, continuing full employment without inflation will result in a higher share for labor than will occur in an occasional period of full employment or one where permanent full employment and constant inflation go hand in hand. While we are inclined [to believe] that union wage pressures do not cause inflation, still the governmental policies associated with New Deal unionism may, and inflation does, cut labor's relative share.

Full employment yields the unions a more favorable environment in which to bargain for money wages but one in which, while they are given an opportunity to chase, they cannot catch the employers. They must be content with catching, in terms of shares, the recipients of rent and of interest, and perhaps also their own members. In fact the chief beneficiary of New Deal unionism, in terms of shares (unless one separates out the share of the previously unemployed which, of course, goes up enormously), is entrepreneurial income. With their policies of the standard rate and full employment, unionism of our first two types might be viewed as the protector of profits.

The relative share, of course, is less important than the real absolute share and the latter rises for labor with the movement from less than full employment to full employment, although it may fall slightly with inflation.

Improvement Unionism · The policy of improvement unionism, as we have defined it, seeks to tie wages closely to the cost of living and to the increase in physical productivity. Wages tend to follow the cost of living and productivity in any event. This policy, by calling for quick and automatic adjustments, reduces the lag. Thus labor's share would tend to fall slightly less than it otherwise would on the upswing and rise slightly less (assuming the escalator clause is allowed to work downward as well as upward) on the downswing. Assuming, however, a full employment economy without inflation, the net results, as compared with what otherwise might happen, would probably be negligible.

The policy probably, on balance, slightly favors chronic inflation by reducing lags, although Ross and Reder have suggested that it will make the swings in both directions more violent.[1] It certainly favors inflation if unions obtain provisions calling for overcompensation for cost-of-living rises and increases in physical productivity. If such a policy of overcompensation becomes generalized over the whole economy, as it did in Finland, and was effectively enforced, the share of labor would have to rise at the expense of some other segment.

The policy of improvement unionism may also result in a heightened public consciousness of inflation and thus in greater public measures to control it or to reduce its customary effects on the distribution of real income, as through the introduction of the universal escalator.

More generally, however, this is a policy designed not so much to catch the employers as to prevent them from running farther away. Individual employers, of course, can run away farther by having their prices advance faster than prices generally or by raising the productivity of their workers more than the general rise in productivity, but employers in totality cannot.

Direct-controls Unionism · The essence of this policy is direct price control by government. At least in the short run, profit margins can be held steady in an inflationary period or even squeezed, if enforcement is adequate, and the share of labor maintained or raised. By holding down rents, the share of labor can further be advantaged. Under this policy, with the government holding on to him, unionism can catch the employer and

1. Arthur M. Ross, "The General Motors Wage Agreement of 1948," and M.W. Reder, "The Significance of the 1948 General Motors Agreement," *Review of Economics and Statistics*, February, 1949.

take some profits from him, although there may be some cost in volume of employment or size of total output.

Managerial Unionism · The program of this type of unionism is to control the distribution of income within the plant or, more usually, within the industry. The specific method may be an all-or-none bargain which obligates the employers to a certain specified wage bill (a given number of employees at a set wage rate) if he is to operate at all. This certainly can cut into profits, as compared with the customary rule of flexibility in the number of employees. The employer, however, may be able to escape the impact of the all-or-none bargain by raising prices or by increasing the output of his labor force.

A second method is direct profit sharing. Here the employer can only regain the original amount of profit he obtained by increasing the total amount, since some of the profit must be shared with his employees. A third device is partial or complete participation in the direction of the industry: the determination of prices and of output and the distribution of the gross returns. Instances even exist where the employers are given a general ceiling on their incomes and, if this ceiling is pierced, the compensation of employees is raised in one fashion or another. The incentive for efficiency, under such arrangements, lies more with the employees than with the employers. This kind of policy is very limited in its actual application, but there is no doubt that under it, given enough power to the union, shares can be affected; labor can receive more than its marginal revenue product.

Labor Party Unionism · This policy relies on taxation and on subvention to affect not the income received in the primary distribution, which we have been discussing up until now, but rather the income retained after secondary distribution has taken place. Through progressive taxation and subsidies, the real income available to labor can be raised as compared with that of originally more highly rewarded elements in the population. Here at last the employer can really be caught, although perhaps not as much as might first appear. Goods and services are taken out of the market place and given to wage and salary earners with the cost financed by taxes bearing heavily on other segments of the population.

AMERICAN AND BRITISH EXPERIENCE

American historical experience is consistent with the suggested impacts of these different union programs. This experience may be summarized as follows:

1. Employee compensation as a share of income originating within the business sector of the economy, after allowing for interindustry shifts in weights, has been quite stable over substantial periods of time. It was virtually unchanged from 1929 to 1950.[2]

2. This share was higher in depression (1930–1933) and recession (1938) than in more prosperous periods.

3. During wartime inflation this share sank a bit but rose later in the one area where price control was most effective—nonfarm corporations.

4. This share rose in 1945–1947 when corporation profits were depressed by reconversion and when unions were unusually aggressive.

5. After adjustments for allocable taxes on income, compensation of employees rose more comparatively from 1929 to 1950 than did other shares. The great loser, after taxes, was the share going to corporate profits.

6. Labor's share of income, industry by industry, has fared no more favorably in unionized industries than in nonunion. Stigler notes that "it is possible that the unions succeeded in increasing the share of labor income in total income." He shows that wages and salaries as a percentage of income originating in selected manufacturing industries went up slightly from 1929 to 1947 in unionized industries while it went down slightly for all manufacturing. However, had he taken 1929 to 1950 he would have found both figures declining substantially and in about the same amount, which would have implied a different conclusion.[3] Levinson may also have been misled by his selection of a ter-

2. Edward F. Denison, 'Distribution of National Income," *Survey of Current Business*, June, 1952. (The data for headings 1 through 5 are all from Denison.) Over the past century, however, labor's share of national income has gained at the expense of farm income. (See Simon Kuznets, *Uses of National Income in Peace and War* [National Bureau of Economic Research, 1942].)

3. *Op. cit.*, p. 259. The pertinent figures are for unionized industry: 1929 (69.1), 1947 (70.1), 1950 (61.7); and for all manufacturing: 1929 (73.1), 1947 (71.5), 1950 (66.1).

minal year. He found that the "union" industrial groups showed a gain in the share of employee compensation (excluding compensation of corporate officers) while the "nonunion" industrial groups remained approximately unchanged between 1929 and 1947. Yet had he taken 1929 and 1951, he would have found a different situation. Over that period, the share of the union groups remained approximately unchanged while the share of the nonunion groups showed a gain. Our own investigations (conducted by Melvin K. Bers) show no significant relationship between the degree of unionization and labor's share, industry group by industry group.

7. Degree of unionization by metropolitan area is not significantly related to labor's share of manufacturing income in these same areas according to our own calculations.

The conclusion from this record is that trade-unionism in the United States to date has had no important effect on labor's share of national income except as (1) it has encouraged an employee-oriented national economic policy with heavy emphasis on full employment (which has served to reduce the share of labor), (2) it has supported effective price control, (3) it has put wage pressure on employers temporarily unable to recapture profits (the special case of the reconversion period when output was limited and the administered prices for durable consumers' goods were rising comparatively slowly), and (4) it has furthered progressive income taxes. There is no evidence of any significant effect through normal collective bargaining. The American experience throws no light on the performance of two of our six types of union programs (improvement unionism and managerial unionism) because they were not widespread enough to have a noticeable impact.

The British history is different in detail but not in essentials. The available data are, however, much more adequate for analytical purposes and cover a far longer period. They may be summarized as follows:

1. The share of wages (not employee compensation) has risen very slightly since 1870, from a little under to a little over 40 percent; but the proportion of workers among the gainfully employed has gone down substantially. As a result, the average income of wage-earners has gained more than that of the rest of the population. This comparative gain has not been at the

expense of profits but rather initially of rent and more recently of salaries. Some of the latter comparative gain may be due to the rising skill level of manual workers and the declining skill level of salaried workers.

2. The share of wages over the cycle has not varied much; sometimes it has gone up slightly and sometimes down slightly. In the Great Depression it rose only very moderately. The rise in employee compensation as a share in the United States during a depression may be due largely to the inclusion of salaried workers whose rates are probably cut less and whose employment most certainly is. One would expect the wage share itself to rise less in Britain than in the United States in the Great Depression both because there is a lower capital-to-labor ratio there and because the amplitude of the fluctuation was not as great.

3. Unionism, according to the excellent study of Phelps Brown and Hart, has had an upward-forcing impact on the share of wages only when the unions have been aggressive and the employers faced a "hard" market, so they could not escape easily and quickly through higher prices. Phelps Brown and Hart note that in the United States the market is more protected and thus more likely to be "soft," allowing employers to escape. Perhaps, also, British unions have been more aggressive historically (although they curbed their aggressiveness after World War II with a policy of wage restraint) and particularly in times of hard markets. In the United States, strong trade-unionism and soft markets have gone closely together. The American employer may also have had a greater chance to evade wage advances through labor-saving innovations. Hard markets are likely to be particularly hard for agricultural products and thus some of the gain for wage-earners is at the expense of agricultural producers; although labor's share has risen, under these conditions, also within the nonagricultural segment of the economy taken by itself.

4. The share of wages remained constant in Britain during World War II, probably, in part, because of the more effective price control.

5. A substantial increase has taken place, as compared with the period prior to World War II, in the real income, after direct taxes, of wage-earners as compared with other elements in the population. Social expenditures for food and health, however,

have been largely offset by higher taxes on beer, tobacco, and other purchases; so that the wage-earners have made no net gain from these subsidies. This British experience suggests two modifications of the conclusion drawn from the American record. First, wage-earners may gain at the expense of salaried workers. Second, full employment probably reduces the share of wages much less than the share of all employees, and unions are particularly concerned with the share of wages.

CONCLUSION

Samuel Butler once observed that "life is the art of drawing sufficient conclusions from insufficient premises." This is too often the task of the economist. He seeks answers to important questions which lend themselves to no sure response. So it is here. We have, however, ventured a reply to our question: Can trade-unionism affect distributive shares? Part of the answer is that, under certain conditions, it can. It can reduce labor's share through the furtherance of a policy of continuing full employment and perhaps also through the application of the standard rate. It can raise labor's share, in particular, through standard collective bargaining when employers cannot quickly escape; or through support of the application of effective price controls; or, in terms of kept income, through the encouragement of progressive taxation and subventions.

The other part of the answer is that, while it can raise labor's share, it cannot raise it by very much. In the United States, to date, the impact has been minimal. The power of trade-unionism, to revert to Galbraith's terminology, has been apparently countervailing and not original. One can only speculate about what might have happened if this countervailing power had not developed; but the American worker, in its absence, certainly would not have been condemned to a share so grossly below what one might expect as are the poor South African workers, as shown in Paul Douglas' statistics. In Great Britain, on the other hand, through what might be viewed as original political power, a significant redistribution has taken place. . . .

Part three Inflation, Unemployment, and Hours of Work

Wage Behavior and the Cost-inflation Problem

WILLIAM G. BOWEN

This essay, written expressly for this volume, is based on a lecture given in the basic economics course at Princeton University and on several of the author's publications dealing with wages and inflation, especially The Wage Price Issue *and* Wage Behavior in the Postwar Period.

The role of wage behavior in the inflationary process has been one of the most hotly debated issues of the postwar years, both in this country and abroad. This is a new development. Prior to the end of World War II most discussions of inflation paid little, if any, attention to wage determination. Inflation was analyzed mainly in terms of changes in the stock of money and in aggregate spending relative to the supply of goods and services. Needless to say, it has long been recognized that increased demand for goods and services leads to increased demand for labor, and that inflationary pressures originating on the demand side have effects on money wages, which in turn affect prices. Recognition of these relationships has led to the adoption of anti-inflationary labor-market policies, especially in wartime, when many governments have instituted wage (and price) controls. In most situations in which wage controls have been employed, however, policymakers have tended to see an excess of demand over supply as the root problem, and to assume that labor markets play a rather passive, transmission-belt role in the inflationary process.

When World War II ended, the inflationary pressures which accompanied it did not end, although they abated considerably. Economists in many Western European countries and in the

United States began to speak of a "new" type of inflation, commonly referred to as "cost inflation." While there are almost as many versions of cost inflation as there are economists who write on the subject, all versions refer, often loosely, to situations in which prices are pushed up from the cost side (cost-push) rather than pulled up from the demand side (demand-pull), and all assign to wage behavior a much more active role than it plays in demand-inflation models.

A SIMPLE COST-INFLATION MODEL

Let us consider the sequence of events in one very simple model of the cost-inflation process. The first component of the model is a wage-determination assertion which states that, in the absence of excess demand for labor, the collective-bargaining process generates wage increases which are greater than increases in productivity. As a result, unit labor costs rise.[1] Next comes a price-determination assertion which states that businessmen price on some kind of cost-plus basis, and that therefore they will respond to increases in unit labor costs by raising product prices. The third, and last, assertion is the monetary–fiscal policy assertion: those responsible for monetary-fiscal policies will take whatever expansionary steps are necessary to enable consumers to continue to buy roughly the same quantity of goods at the higher prices now being charged.

1. At this juncture it may be helpful to some readers if we illustrate the arithmetic of the wage-productivity–unit-labor-cost relationship, since it occupies such an important place both in the model of the cost-inflation process and in the policy debate concerning the famous "guidelines" formulated by the Council of Economic Advisers. To begin with a definition, "unit labor cost" (*ULC*) is just what its name implies: the dollar cost of the labor needed to produce one unit of output. It can be expressed as $ULC = \frac{W}{P}$, where *W* is the wage rate per hour and *P* is "productivity" (output per man hour). Thus, if the wage rate were \$1.00 and if one man could produce 5 units of output in one hour, unit labor cost would be $\frac{\$1.00}{5} = \$.20$. It follows from this definitional relationship that if both wages per hour and productivity increase at the same percentage rate, unit labor cost will be unchanged. Suppose, for instance, that both *W* and *P* go up 40 percent; then, $ULC = \frac{\$1.40}{7} = \$.20$. The basic point is that increases in wage payments per hour lead to increases in unit labor costs only if productivity increases at a slower rate than wages per hour.

FIG. 1. *The Rate of Change of Money Wages Related to the Level of Unemployment, 1948–1963*

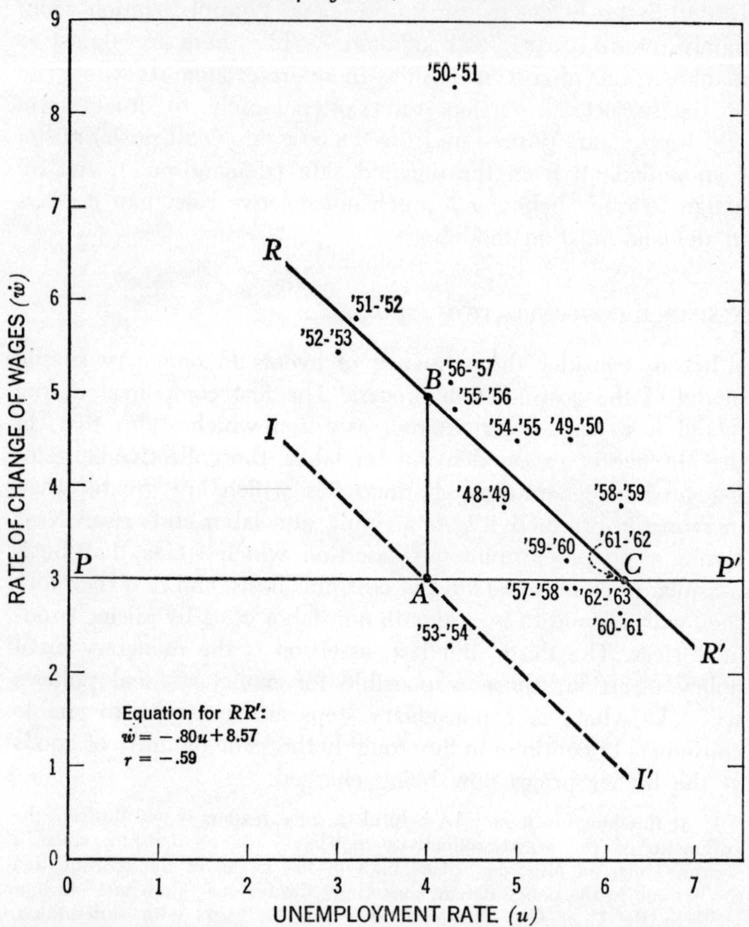

The "rate of change of wages" (w) is, more accurately, the percentage rate of change in gross average hourly earnings in manufacturing from one year to the next. "Unemployment" (u) is the average percentage of the civilian labor force unemployed over each two-year span. Thus, $w_{55\text{-}56} = \dfrac{w_{56} - w_{55}}{w_{55}}$ and $u_{55\text{-}56} = \dfrac{u_{55} + u_{56}}{2}$. The reasons for aligning the wage and and unemployment series in this manner are explained at length in W. G. Bowen and R. A. Berry, "Unemployment Conditions and Movements of the Money Wage Level," *Review of Economics and Statistics*, May 1963, pp. 171–172. The data are from the Economic Report of the President, 1964, pp. 230, 242.

If the figures for the Korean war ('50–'51) are omitted, the coefficient of correlation r goes up to $-.69$ and the regression equation becomes $w = -.72u + 7.51$.

This simple model has the virtue of calling attention to the interaction between the cost-push and demand-pull aspects of almost any inflationary process. That is, while in the case being considered here it is a large wage increase which initiates the process (conceptually, it could just as easily be an autonomous increase in profit margins or in the prices of imported raw materials), "appropriate" monetary- or fiscal-policy responses are necessary to prevent the process from being choked off for lack of sufficient demand. Suppose, for instance, that monetary and fiscal policymakers adopted the policy of not allowing total money spending to rise, no matter what happened. In this situation, a given increase in the price level would require an offsetting reduction in the quantity of goods sold, a derived decrease in the demand for labor, and an increase in unemployment. If wages continued to rise more rapidly than productivity, the cycle would repeat itself and unemployment would increase still more. At what point (if ever) the growing volume of unemployment would dampen wage increases sufficiently to halt the upward pressure on the price level is an empirical question, to which we shall turn shortly.

In the real world, it is of course unlikely that monetary and fiscal policymakers would be willing to tolerate increasing unemployment. Probably they would ease credit and allow money incomes and money spending to increase sufficiently to permit the same quantity of goods to be purchased as before, thus validating the increase in the price level and setting the stage for another round.

For our present purposes, the important point to note about this cost-inflation model is that it forces monetary and fiscal policymakers to wrestle with a dilemma: restrictive policies mean unemployment, but expansionary policies facilitate further rounds of inflation. For this reason, this has been called the "dilemma model" of the inflationary process.

Could things really happen this way? The answer is clearly "yes," this kind of cost-inflation model, when carefully stated, is internally consistent. The more difficult—and more interesting—questions, however, are: What kinds of evidence can be used to determine whether in fact we have experienced a significant degree of cost inflation? What does the relevant evidence show? What are the policy implications?

THE EVIDENCE

How can we identify cost inflation when we see it? This is not an easy question, and the interaction between cost and demand elements even in the simple model of the cost-inflation process described above makes empirical identification very difficult.

Our main concern here is the wage-behavior aspect of the cost-inflation problem. From this perspective the best measurement approach consists of looking at the relation between unemployment and the rate of change of money wages. This relationship as it has existed in the United States, from 1948 to 1963, is depicted in Figure 1.

The first thing to note about this scatter of points is that relatively *low* levels of unemployment have tended to be associated with relatively *large* increases in average hourly earnings. We can obtain a more precise notion of the character of the relationship by fitting a straight line to the scatter of points (*RR′*). The negative slope of *RR′* comes as no surprise, since in periods of low unemployment (and tight labor markets), competition by employers for labor leads to larger wage increases than in periods of high unemployment and relatively abundant labor. The bargaining position of a union is of course stronger when unemployment is low and the demand for the employer's product brisk than when the converse conditions hold. Collective bargaining does not operate independently of economic conditions. This simple scatter diagram indicates that it is wrong to suppose that in our economy wages are completely unresponsive to the level of unemployment.

This is certainly not to say, however, that institutional considerations, such as the extent of union organization, employer organization and the basic characteristics of our labor markets, have no influence on wage behavior. In Figure 1, these institutional characteristics can be thought of as influencing the *position* of the *RR′* curve. If unions were nonexistent, if employers always paid the lowest wage consistent with short-run profit maximization, and if labor were perfectly mobile, then wages would rise less rapidly (and fall more readily) at given levels of unemployment, and the entire *RR′* schedule might shift down to, say, *II′*.

We must also emphasize that, as the dispersion of observations for the individual years around the fitted line testifies, wage behavior is certainly not such a simple phenomenon that all variations in rates of increase can be explained in terms of movements along a stable *RR'* curve associated with variations in the level of unemployment. Other factors—such as the direction in which unemployment is changing, the level of profits, the movement of the consumer price index, overtime provisions, and the timing of key negotiations—also exert influence. Furthermore, as the effect of the outbreak of the Korean war on price and wage increases between 1950 and 1951 illustrates, sudden changes in expectations can have a pronounced short-run effect.

We could speculate further on the significance of this scatter of points for wage determination in the U.S. economy, but it is more important to return to the basic question posed at the beginning of this section: the relevance of wage behavior for the cost-inflation controversy. As noted earlier, cost inflation poses a serious policy problem because it implies that we may experience inflation even during periods of significant unemployment. From the standpoint of the contribution of wage behavior to this problem, we saw earlier that unit labor costs increase only when wages go up more rapidly than productivity. Therefore, to measure the contribution of wage-setting mechanisms to cost inflation, it is necessary to examine the movements of money wages relative to productivity at various levels of unemployment.

To translate this proposition into graphic terms, let us assume, for the sake of simplicity, that productivity increases at the rate of 3 percent per year regardless of the level of unemployment. The horizontal line *PP'* on Figure 1 reflects this assumption. The vertical distance between *RR'* and *PP'* indicates the approximate amount by which unit labor costs have risen at various levels of unemployment. At 4 percent unemployment, for instance, where average hourly earnings have tended to increase at the rate of about 5 percent per year, assuming a 3-percent increase in productivity, there is about a 2 percent increase in unit labor costs, measured roughly by line *AB*. (Strictly speaking, if our wage index increases from 100 to 105 and our productivity index increases from 100 to 103, unit labor costs increase not by 2 percent but by $\frac{105}{103} = 1.94$ percent.) Figure 1 also suggests that, on the average, it has taken an unemployment rate of slightly more than 6 percent to prevent labor costs from rising at all. So, unless we are prepared to regard 6-percent unemployment as "full employment," we must conclude that, from the wage-setting side, our economy has been subject to "cost inflation," in the sense that unit labor costs have tended to rise before full employment has been reached.

How much of a downward shift in the *RR′* curve would be required to eliminate the policy dilemma altogether depends on how one defines "full employment." If we accept the conservative goal of 4-percent unemployment, then *RR′* would need to pass through point *A* (as *II′* does), and the extent to which our present situation departs from this "ideal" can be measured in terms of the (average) distance between *II′* and *RR′*. A simpler index can be obtained by calculating the area of triangle *ABC*. This can be done in terms of objective data (we don't need to make assumptions about the exact slope of *II′*). The area of this triangle is intuitively meaningful, in that it is the sum of the *increases* in unit labor costs associated with all levels of unemployment above the "full"-employment level.

Thinking about cost inflation in these terms also provides us with a way of comparing our postwar experience with earlier experiences. In principle, we could fit a line like *RR′* to the observations for earlier years and then compare these results (and the area of the triangle analogous to *ABC*) with the postwar results. Unfortunately, however, the economic history of the United States during much of the first half of the twentieth century was so replete with "unusual" events that many observations have to be discarded. The experience of the 1930s for instance, is strictly *sui generis*, as is the experience with wage controls during World War II. The figures for the first two decades of the 1900s (excluding the World War I years) are less subject to extreme abnormalities, and a comparison of this period with the postwar years does yield several interesting findings. First of all, even in the early 1900s, before the advent of large industrial unions, average hourly earnings tended to increase faster than productivity when the unemployment rate was below 6 percent. So, the limited evidence that is available indicates that cost inflation, viewed from the wage side, is by no means a distinctly new phenomenon. The data also suggest, however, that at comparable rates of unemployment average hourly earnings in manufacturing tended to rise more rapidly in the postwar years than in the period prior to 1930. Postwar wage behavior does seem to be somewhat less conducive to the simultaneous achievement of price stability and high-level employment than wage behavior in the early part of the century.

POLICY IMPLICATIONS

In this country, main reliance has been placed on aggregate demand measures (monetary and fiscal policies) in our efforts to achieve a reasonable degree of price stability and relatively high employment. In terms of Figure 1, these tools can be thought of as moving us along a given wage-unemployment-reaction curve (approximated by *RR′*) to whatever point seems most desirable from the standpoint of society's preferences for low unemployment *vs.* price stability.[2]

The menu of choices given by the position of the *RR′* curve is such that, over a considerable range, the makers of monetary and fiscal policies must expect to face both an unemployment problem and some upward pressure from the cost side on the price level. Furthermore, the slope of *RR′* implies that by taking steps to ease one problem, they will aggravate the other problem. In short, the policy dilemma suggested by the simple cost-inflation model is real enough.[3]

2. Actually, the specific mix of monetary and fiscal policies used in a given situation will also have some influence on the shape and position of *RR′*. For instance, if we were to increase aggregate demand by means of a substantial increase in public expenditures for space exploration, we would be much more likely to encounter bottlenecks at relatively high levels of over-all unemployment than if the same increase in aggregate demand were brought about by a widely diffused tax cut. Thus, if the increased space-expenditure route were taken, the increase in aggregate demand would probably lead to a somewhat larger increase in wages (because of the shortage of space workers) and a somewhat smaller increase in employment than if the tax-cut route had been taken. In terms of Figure 1, *RR′* would be farther to the right and somewhat steeper in the space-expenditure case than in the tax-cut case.

3. To be more precise, the evidence presented here indicates that the dilemma is a real one provided that the upward pressure on prices exerted by increases in production-worker labor costs in manufacturing is not offset by decreases in other labor costs, in nonlabor costs, in profit margins, or in the prices of imported goods. Conceptually, these other elements could, of course, worsen as well as improve the menu of policy choices.

It would be wrong to infer that monetary and fiscal policies cannot be used to halt "cost inflation." A sufficient reduction in aggregate demand would presumably move us down the *RR′* line to point *C*, where unit labor costs are stable. But the important point is that by taking such action, we would allow substantial unemployment to develop at the same time. Many people have commented on the relative stability of labor costs and prices in the U.S. over the last few years, but they sometimes fail to note that relative stability has been accompanied by considerable unemployment.

This policy dilemma cannot be solved by wishing it away, or by saying that to admit that there can be a conflict of goals is to display a "lack of faith in America." Given the present nature of our labor and product markets, the makers of monetary and fiscal policies must face up to the need for making hard-headed choices. How bad is a 1-percent increase in the price level vis-à-vis an additional 1 to 1½ percent of the labor force unemployed?[4]

In addition to trying to find the optimal point on the present *RR′* line, policymakers may also try to shift the entire line to a more advantageous position. Proposals to reduce the market power of unions and corporations and to return to a more atomistic type of economy may have this as one objective. It is well to remember, however, that the link between union size and union power may be weak and, moreover, that the relationship between union power and the size of wage settlements may be more complex than it at first appears to be. In fact, some scholars have suggested that we move in the other direction, that we emulate some foreign countries by encouraging more centralization of bargaining so that the national interest will loom larger in the thinking of the negotiators. In evaluating proposals for institutional reform, it is very important to remember that participation in wage-setting is only one of the functions of unions (probably not the most important), and that a proposal designed to weaken a union's bargaining power in the

4. In arriving at one's own answer to this question, it is necessary to consider not only the relative costs of inflation and unemployment but also the accuracy of our measures of these phenomena. As Albert Rees indicates in his paper in this volume (pp. 95–105), there are reasons for thinking that the price indices exaggerate the true increases in prices because of their inability to allow fully for quality improvements.

wage arena may also weaken its ability to protect its members from arbitrary treatment.

Union-busting and trust-busting are certainly not the only possible ways of seeking to shift *RR′* down to a lower level. Wage controls can also be used, and have been in wartime, though they raise serious problems of administration, allocation, and equity. The exhortations of public officials and the publication of "guideposts" for wage- and price-setting constitute a less extreme, though nonetheless controversial, approach to the problem, as other articles in this volume indicate. As noted earlier, shortages of workers in particular areas or with particular skills can also put upward pressure on labor costs (by creating "bottlenecks"), and in this connection mention should be made of the increasing efforts in this country to retrain workers and promote mobility.

The purpose of this essay has not been to advocate one policy or another but to clarify the issues and present some relevant evidence as to the trade-offs which exist at the present time. In conclusion, however, I do wish to express the following personal judgments. (1) The cost-inflation problem, while real, has been exaggerated, and it is not serious enough to justify radical institutional surgery. (2) Efforts to increase the adaptability of the labor force are all to the good and will help somewhat to make high employment and price stability more compatible. (3) Carefully directed exhortations of public officials are not likely to do much harm and may even do some good. (4) Finally, what is most important at the present time is an attitude of realism and a willingness to accept somewhat greater risks of inflation than we accepted in the 1957–1963 period in order to reduce what I regard as an intolerably high level of unemployment.

Guideposts for Noninflationary Wage and Price Behavior

COUNCIL OF ECONOMIC ADVISERS

The Council of Economic Advisers was established to advise the President by the Employment Act of 1946. Of all the words published since then by various Councils, none has been so widely quoted and discussed as this statement from the January 1962 Economic Report of the President.

THERE ARE IMPORTANT segments of the economy where firms are large or employees well-organized, or both. In these sectors, private parties may exercise considerable discretion over the terms of wage bargains and price decisions. Thus, at least in the short run, there is considerable room for the exercise of private power and a parallel need for the assumption of private responsibility.

Individual wage and price decisions assume national importance when they involve large numbers of workers and large amounts of output directly, or when they are regarded by large segments of the economy as setting a pattern. Because such decisions affect the progress of the whole economy, there is legitimate reason for public interest in their content and consequences. An informed public, aware of the significance of major wage bargains and price decisions, and equipped to judge for itself their compatibility with the national interest, can help to create an atmosphere in which the parties to such decisions will exercise their powers responsibly.

How is the public to judge whether a particular wage-price decision is in the national interest? No simple test exists, and it is not possible to set out systematically all of the many considerations which bear on such a judgment. However, since the question is of prime importance to the strength and progress of the American economy, it deserves widespread public discussion and clarification of the issues. What follows is intended as a contribution to such a discussion.

Mandatory controls in peacetime over the outcomes of wage negotiations and over individual price decisions are neither desirable in the American tradition nor practical in a diffuse and decentralized continental economy. Free collective bargaining is the vehicle for the achievement of contractual agreements on wages, fringes, and working conditions, as well as on the "web of rules" by which a large segment of industry governs the performance of work and the distribution of rewards. Similarly, final price decisions lie—and should continue to lie—in the hands of individual firms. It is, however, both desirable and practical that discretionary decisions on wages and prices recognize the national interest in the results. The guideposts suggested here as aids to public understanding are not concerned primarily with the relation of employers and employees to each other, but rather with their joint relation to the rest of the economy.

WAGES, PRICES, AND PRODUCTIVITY

If all prices remain stable, all hourly labor costs may increase as fast as economy-wide productivity without, for that reason alone, changing the relative share of labor and nonlabor incomes in total output. At the same time, each kind of income increases steadily in absolute amount. If hourly labor costs increase at a slower rate than productivity, the share of nonlabor incomes will grow or prices will fall, or both. Conversely, if hourly labor costs increase more rapidly than productivity, the share of labor incomes in the total product will increase or prices will rise, or both. It is this relationship among long-run economy-wide productivity, wages, and prices which makes the rate of productivity change an important benchmark for noninflationary wage and price behavior.

Productivity is a *guide* rather than a *rule* for appraising wage and price behavior for several reasons. First, there are a number of problems involved in measuring productivity change, and a number of alternative measures are available. Second, there is nothing immutable in fact or in justice about the distribution of the total product between labor and nonlabor incomes. Third, the pattern of wages and prices among industries is and should be responsive to forces other than changes in productivity.

Annual Rates of Growth of Output per Man-hour, 1909 to 1960 (based on establishment series)

Industry series	Average annual percentage change [a]			
	1909 to 1960	1947 to 1960	1947 to 1954	1954 to 1960
Total private economy	2.4	3.0	3.5	2.6
Nonagriculture	2.1	2.4	2.7	2.2
Nonmanufacturing	[b]	2.2	2.6	1.9
Manufacturing	[b]	2.8	2.9	2.9
Manufacturing corrected for varying rates of capacity utilization	[b]	2.8	2.8	3.1

[a] Computed from least squares trend of the logarithms of the output per man-hour indexes.

[b] Not available.

SOURCES: Department of Labor and Council of Economic Advisers.

ALTERNATIVE MEASURES OF PRODUCTIVITY

If the rate of growth of productivity over time is to serve as a useful benchmark for wage and price behavior, there must be some meeting of minds about the appropriate methods of measuring the trend rate of increase in productivity, both for industry as a whole and for individual industries. This is a large and complex subject and there is much still to be learned. The most that can be done at present is to give some indication of orders of magnitude, and of the range within which most plausible measures are likely to fall (see table above).

There are a number of conceptual problems in connection with productivity measurement which can give rise to differences in estimates of its rate of growth. Three important conceptual problems are the following:

1. Over what time interval should productivity trends be measured? Very short intervals may give excessive weight to business-cycle movements in productivity, which are not the relevant standards for wage behavior. Very long intervals may hide significant breaks in trends; indeed in the United States—and in other countries as well—productivity appears to have risen more rapidly since the end of the Second World War than before. It would be wholly inappropriate for wage behavior in the 1960s to be governed by events long in the past. On the other hand, productivity in the total private economy appears to have advanced less rapidly in the second half of the postwar

period than in the first.

2. Even for periods of intermediate length, it is desirable to segregate the trend movements in productivity from those that reflect business-cycle forces. Where the basic statistical materials are available, this problem can be handled by an analytical separation of trend effects and the effects of changes in the rate of capacity utilization.

3. Even apart from such difficulties, there often exist alternative statistical measures of output and labor input. The alternatives may differ conceptually or may simply be derived from different statistical sources. A difficult problem of choice may emerge, unless the alternative measures happen to give similar results.

Selected measures of the rate of growth of productivity in different sectors of the economy for different time periods are shown in the table. Several measures are given because none of the single figures is clearly superior for all purposes.

THE SHARE OF LABOR INCOME

The proportions in which labor and nonlabor incomes share the product of industry have not been immutable throughout American history, nor can they be expected to stand forever where they are today. It is desirable that labor and management should bargain explicitly about the distribution of the income of particular firms or industries. It is, however, undesirable that they should bargain implicitly about the general price level. Excessive wage settlements which are paid for through price increases in major industries put direct pressure on the general price level and produce spillover and imitative effects throughout the economy. Such settlements may fail to redistribute income within the industry involved; rather they redistribute income between that industry and other segments of the economy through the mechanism of inflation.

PRICES AND WAGES IN INDIVIDUAL INDUSTRIES

What are the guideposts which may be used in judging whether a particular price or wage decision may be inflationary? The desired objective is a stable price level, within which particular prices rise, fall, or remain stable in response to economic pressures. Hence, price stability within any particular industry is not necessarily a correct guide to price and wage decisions in that industry. It is possible, however, to describe in broad outline a set of guides which, if followed, would preserve over-all price stability while still allowing sufficient flexibility to accommodate objectives of efficiency and equity. These are not arbitrary guides. They describe—briefly and no doubt incompletely—how prices and wage rates would behave in a smoothly functioning competitive economy operating near full employment. Nor do they constitute a mechanical formula for determining whether a particular price or wage decision is inflationary. They will serve their purpose if they suggest to the interested public a useful way of approaching the appraisal of such a decision.

If, as a point of departure, we assume no change in the relative shares of labor and nonlabor incomes in a particular industry, then a general guide may be advanced for noninflationary wage behavior, and another for noninflationary price behavior. Both guides, as will be seen, are only first approximations.

The general guide for noninflationary wage behavior is that the rate of increase in wage rates (including fringe benefits) in each industry be equal to the trend rate of over-all productivity increase. General acceptance of this guide would maintain stability of labor cost per unit of output for the economy as a whole —though not of course for individual industries.

The general guide for noninflationary price behavior calls for price reduction if the industry's rate of productivity increase exceeds the overall rate—for this would mean declining unit labor costs; it calls for an appropriate increase in price if the opposite relationship prevails; and it calls for stable prices if the two rates of productivity increase are equal.

These are advanced as general guideposts. To reconcile them with objectives of equity and efficiency, specific modifications must be made to adapt them to the circumstances of particular industries. If all of these modifications are made, each in the specific circumstances to which it applies, they are consistent with stability of the general price level. Public judgments about the effects on the price level of particular wage or price decisions should take into account the modifications as well as the general guides. The most important modifications are the following:

1. Wage rate increases would exceed the general guide rate in an industry which would otherwise be unable to attract sufficient labor; or in which wage rates are exceptionally low compared with the range of wages earned elsewhere by similar labor, because the bargaining position of workers has been weak in particular local labor markets.

2. Wage rate increases would fall short of the general guide rate in an industry which could not provide jobs for its entire labor force even in times of generally full employment; or in which wage rates are exceptionally high compared with the range of wages earned elsewhere by similar labor, because the bargaining position of workers has been especially strong.

3. Prices would rise more rapidly, or fall more slowly, than indicated by the general guide rate in an industry in which the level of profits was insufficient to attract the capital required to finance a needed expansion in capacity; or in which costs other than labor costs had risen.

4. Prices would rise more slowly, or fall more rapidly, than indicated by the general guide in an industry in which the relation of productive capacity to full employment demand shows the desirability of an outflow of capital from the industry; or in which costs other than labor costs have fallen; or in which excessive market power has resulted in rates of profit substantially higher than those earned elsewhere on investments of comparable risk.

It is a measure of the difficulty of the problem that even these complex guideposts leave out of account several important considerations. Although output per man-hour rises mainly in response to improvements in the quantity and quality of capital goods with which employees are equipped, employees are often able to improve their performance by means within their own control. It is obviously in the public interest that incentives be preserved which would reward employees for such efforts.

Also, in connection with the use of measures of over-all productivity gain as benchmarks for wage increases, it must be borne in mind that average hourly labor costs often change through the process of up- or down-grading, shifts between wage and salaried employment, and other forces. Such changes may either add to or subtract from the increment which is available for wage increases under the over-all productivity guide.

Finally, it must be reiterated that collective bargaining within an industry over the division of the proceeds between labor and nonlabor income is not necessarily disruptive of over-all price stability. The relative shares can change within the bounds of noninflationary price behavior. But when a disagreement between management and labor is resolved by passing the bill to the rest of the economy, the bill is paid in depreciated currency to the ultimate advantage of no one.

It is no accident that productivity is the central guidepost for wage settlements. Ultimately, it is rising output per man hour which must yield the ingredients of a rising standard of living. Growth in productivity makes it possible for real wages and real profits to rise side by side.

Rising productivity is the foundation of the country's leadership of the free world, enabling it to earn in world competition the means to discharge its commitments overseas. Rapid advance of productivity is the key to stability of the price level as money incomes rise, to fundamental improvement in the balance of international payments, and to growth in the nation's capacity to meet the challenges of the 1960s at home and abroad. That is why policy to accelerate economic growth stresses investments in science and technology, plant and equipment, education and training—the basic sources of future gains in productivity.

Restraint and National Wage Policy

ALBERT REES

Albert Rees is professor of economics at the University of Chicago. This paper, which is critical of the Council of Economic Advisers' "guideposts" policy, was first presented at a University of Pennsylvania Industrial Relations Conference in late 1960.

THERE IS WIDE agreement among economists that the United States needs a national policy to guide the movement of wages in an economy committed to reasonably full employment and to the right to collective bargaining. In the absence of such a policy, it is feared that strong unions will contribute to cost-push inflation. There is even surprising unanimity on the content of this national wage policy: the average rate of increase in hourly earnings and fringe benefits (in current dollars) should not exceed the rate of growth of man-hour productivity in the economy as a whole. Such a policy is consistent with the preservation of a stable price level and of the initial distribution of income between wage-earners and others. The policy is to be implemented by the voluntary restraint of the parties to collective bargaining and of those employers who are in a position to set wages unilaterally. In the background lurks the threat that if voluntary restraint is not forthcoming, some sort of government pressures or controls to enforce the policy will be needed. . . .

My most basic objection to the proposed policy is that it is one of extreme conservatism, not in the good sense of upholding principles that have proved their value, but in the empty, negative sense of opposing change simply because it is change. The conservative aspect of the position is, of course, that it views the existing distribution of income as fair and just, a proposition from which most unions and many employers would dissent, for different reasons. What is worse, it assumes that this distribution will continue to be fair and workable under the changed economic conditions of the future.

It is interesting to note how often economic policies designed to insure "fair shares" take the form of freezing historical income or price relationships and attempting to maintain them in changed circumstances. This concept of equity underlies many arbitration decisions that restore or continue historical wage differentials between groups of workers. In an extreme form, it underlies the position that the purchasing power of a bushel of wheat should forever remain as high as it was in the years 1910–1914, though the amount of resources needed to grow a bushel of wheat has fallen dramatically and we are accumulating surpluses faster than we can give them away. It is possible for a wheat farmer or a locomotive fireman, each in his own way, to be as reactionary as any member of the Union League Club when change threatens traditional economic privileges. A wage policy that would link wage changes to the growth of productivity and thus preserve indefinitely the initial distribution of income differs in degree from a parity price policy for farm products, but not in basic spirit.

It might be thought that the parties to collective bargaining have already accepted this kind of a wage policy in many basic industries. Have they not agreed to long-term contracts providing for periodic increases in real wages according to an "annual improvement factor" or some similar formula under another name? A moment's reflection on the history of collective bargaining in these industries will suggest that they have not. When these agreements have been renegotiated, they have provided additional wage increases for particular groups of workers and valuable and expensive improvements in fringe benefits. Real compensation has been tied to a formula only for periods of two, three, or at most five years.

If we remove from the proposed national wage formula the implication that distributive shares are to be frozen, the whole scheme is endangered. Once labor's share of national income is allowed to increase, a rate of wage increase in excess of productivity gains is consistent with price stability, while if the property share of national income is allowed to increase, the "warranted" rate of wage increase becomes too large to prevent inflation. I have no particular reason for holding that at this time labor's share is either too small or too large, but this is very different from saying that the present shares should be permanently enshrined and preserved.

Two arguments have often been advanced in support of the

proposed national wage policy: first, that labor's share has in fact been stable historically, and second, that it is already so large that it cannot get appreciably larger. Neither argument seems convincing. The stability of labor's share if it existed would be more of a statistical and historical accident than the outcome of any permanent economic principle or law. Recent statistical research, especially that of Professor Irving Kravis of the University of Pennsylvania, creates serious doubt that there ever was such stability.[1] Professor Kravis's estimates show a rise in labor's share of national income between the years 1900–1909 and the years 1949–1957 of from 3 to 10 percentage points, depending on the method of estimation that is used. On all methods, much of this rise took place before 1934, or before unions were of appreciable importance in the economy as a whole. Along with the rise in labor's share, Kravis shows a steady fall in the return to capital relative to the price of labor. I see no particular reason to believe that these trends have run their full course and can go no further. However, the position that the shares should not be frozen by policy does not depend on the prediction of a continued rise in labor's share in the absence of such a policy. It would be equally valid if the natural future tendencies of the economy would lead to a rise in the property share.

As we accumulate capital and as incomes rise, as people choose to spend more of their lives in education, in vacations, and in retirement rather than in work, as the taste for being a manager or a scientist rises and that for being a laborer or a housemaid declines, new relationships will have to develop among wages, salaries, and returns to property. Such relationships will seem strange by the standards of today, just as it would be incredible to a man of 1890 to find that a coal miner now earns more than a clerk. But such adjustments are needed to prevent gluts or shortages of capital and labor in various forms, and they cannot always be relied on to take place within a rigid framework of fixed shares. When it is first recognized that these adjustments are taking place, no doubt those who lose by them have always regarded them as unfair. In time, however, new concepts of equity develop around the new income relationships and these in their turn are defended against

1. Irving B. Kravis, "Relative Income Shares in Fact and Theory," *American Economic Review,* XLIX (December 1959), 917–949.

further change.

To be sure, we could formulate a national wage policy that set a "warranted" rate of growth of wages somewhat higher than the rate of growth of productivity, or somewhat lower, and thus implied shifting relative shares. However, any such formula implies some arbitrary projection of past trends into the future, and some arbitrary and centralized judgment about equitable distribution.

All of these difficulties could be put aside if there were some compelling reason for having a national wage policy. In my opinion, there is not. The policy is put forth primarily as a defense against peacetime inflation. This fear of inflation seems to me to be much exaggerated. In the seven years since the end of the Korean War, wholesale prices have advanced about 9 percent and the Consumers Price Index has risen about 11 percent. These would not be intolerably high rates of increase even if they could be taken at face value. After devoting a good deal of time to studying the methods by which our price indexes are constructed, I am convinced that these peacetime increases cannot be taken at face value; except during wars the indexes have important and systematic upward biases that could account for large portions of the measured price rise. Unemployment and the failure to make full use of our resources strike me as more pressing peacetime problems than creeping inflation.

If it is difficult to support the proposed national wage policy in principle, it is even more difficult to see how it would work in practice. No one proposes that wages in each occupation, industry, or locality should rise at exactly the same rate. It is possible to fail to notice that the formula most often proposed would freeze labor's share, but almost everyone has noticed that the uniform application of it would freeze relative wages and that this would have serious effects on the allocation of labor. The remedy proposed is that industries, occupations, and areas that are short of labor or growing rapidly should raise their wages by more than the average rate of increase in productivity, while industries with chronic labor surpluses should raise their wages less than the average or not at all. The basic formula thus provides a rule that is both completely general and completely empty; every actual wage determination can be viewed as an exception to the basic rule in the light of local circumstances. A unified national system of wage controls might eventually be expected to develop criteria for taking all these local circumstances into account, but this would involve a degree of interference with labor markets and collective bargaining that no one has seriously contemplated. As for putting such a policy into effect through voluntary restraint one need only imagine a Secretary of Labor attempting to persuade John L. Lewis in his prime that the United Mine Workers should not demand a wage increase because coal mining had a higher than average rate of unemployment. One can hardly doubt that the reply would have been terse, pungent, and most emphatically negative.

There can be no such thing as a wholly scientific discussion of policy; policy issues inevitably involve the tastes and values of the discussants as well as their reasoning and knowledge. My own tastes incline me strongly against any long-run reliance on voluntary restraint in our kind of political and economic system. We can and must call on individuals and organizations to make certain sacrifices for the general good in time of war, or in the settlement of a few critical emergency strikes. On the other hand, we cannot and should not rely on self-restraint as a permanent factor in the making of most important wage decisions. Our economic system is premised on the belief that if each of us pursues his individual goals in open competition, the general welfare will also be advanced. Similarly, our political system is based on the open competition of parties and interest groups with selfish but incompatible interests, no one of which is able to dominate the whole. These are basically eighteenth century ideas, but they look more rather than less attractive in comparison with the twentieth century ideologies that call on the individual continuously to sacrifice his own goals for the goals of the state.

The application of this to collective bargaining is the view that the main business of a union is to advance the interests of its members and the main business of a company is to earn a return for its stockholders. Of course, this does not mean that these goals can be pursued by fair means or foul, that the parties to bargaining should be free to engage in unethical practices simply because they are not illegal, or that it is wrong for companies or unions to make charitable contributions or to give the time of their leaders to civic causes. Nevertheless, negotiators at a bargaining table are agents, not principals, and if they can reach an agreement consistent with the interests of their principals, it is usually unwise as well as unavailing to ask them to put it aside to conform to the supposed interest of the public.

An analogy from baseball might illuminate this point. Suppose that in a ball park with a very short right-field fence, left-handed pull hitters are reaping a rich harvest of home runs. It would hardly improve the game for the umpire to urge each left-handed batter to bunt in the interests of sportsmanship. It would be far better to move back the fence and let everyone do his best. The policy of restraint seems exactly analogous to asking union leaders to bunt. If the rules of collective bargaining as they are now established result in union wages that are too high or rise too rapidly, then surely the only fair and effective solution is to change the rules. Insofar as we need a national wage policy, it should deal with the methods of setting wages and not with the substance of the determinations. It may occasionally be necessary for government to participate in setting the terms of a wage settlement in the event of an emergency strike, but such occasions should be very rare, probably rarer than they have been in the past. In any event, government participation in the settlement of emergency wage disputes is unlikely to assist a policy of wage restraint. In such situations the overriding interest of the government is in getting the strikers back to work, even if this means putting pressure on employers to make additional concessions.

All experiences with policies of wage restraint during rapid peacetime inflation suggest that they are unworkable. Where unions have exercised restraint, as in Scandinavia, there has nevertheless been a substantial increase in earnings over and above the increase in union rates as a result of the upgrading of labor, the loosening of wage incentive systems, and similar forces. This so-called wage drift is now too widely known and too well documented to require further discussion. In the United States, the experience of the Wage Stabilization Board during the Korean conflict shows that the parties to collective bargaining cannot be induced to use restraint even when the nation is engaged in active if limited warfare. It can be argued that the government did not put enough teeth in its Korean stabilization policies; my own feeling, however, is that more compulsion would have harmed rather than furthered the national interest.

Even the strict wage controls of World War II had such serious drawbacks as to suggest the need for a different approach under similar circumstances, in the unlikely event that similar circumstances can recur in the age of the hydrogen bomb. In World War II we never learned to control the general level of wages without interfering seriously with the kind of wage structure needed to attract and hold labor in areas of critical shortages. For example, essential procurement programs were crippled for lack of foundry parts because of the failure to admit that hot, dirty work in foundries commands a higher wage premium in a period of accute manpower shortages than in the depressed prewar period on which official standards of equity were based.

However, this discussion of wage restraint under demand inflation is not relevant to most of the period since 1953, when concern about national wage policy has been growing. The recent problem is that of "creeping inflation," often identified as cost-push or wage-push inflation as distinguished from demand inflation. Most of the analysis of price rises in this period has involved the role of collective bargaining as a central issue.

To the extent that there have been real, as opposed to measured, increases in the general level of prices during a period of adequate and often redundant labor supply, it is tempting to explain them as a result of wage pressures. Yet it is hard to see how collective bargaining alone could raise the general level of prices more than temporarily. This is not to deny that a convincing theoretical model of a wage-price spiral can be created; indeed, many have been. Rather, it is to say that these models do not fit the institutions and circumstances of the United States during the postwar period.

The salient point to be kept in mind is that collective bargaining covers only one-third of nonagricultural wage and salary workers, and that even within this third there are many workers whose unions do not have any substantial power over wages. When labor markets are tight, the wage patterns set by strong unions are quickly copied by weaker unions and by nonunion employers. This copying probably influences the form and timing of the wage increases more than the amount, since demand forces would justify wage increases in the nonunion sector in any case. However, the spread of union wage patterns to the nonunion sector will be severely limited in periods of loose labor markets, and probably will not extend beyond the immediate vicinity of the original bargain. In more remote parts of the nonunion sector, the effect of union wage increases at such times may be quite the opposite. By limiting the growth of employment in the union sector, the increases can reduce any pressures on nonunion employers to raise wages.

The importance of the nonunion sector of the American economy forces us to reconsider the usual model of the wage-price spiral. This model implies that strong unions will cause either inflation or persistent unemployment, if they raise wages faster than the rate of growth of productivity. Inflation will result if the government is committed to supply the aggregate demand needed to support the higher level of wages and prices. General unemployment will result if the government is committed to price-level stability and fails to provide the needed aggregate demand, or if it mops up any independent increase in aggregate demand created by or simultaneously with the wage increase. (I am considering the Federal Reserve System as part of the government in this discussion.) The unions are thus convicted of causing either inflation or depression, and government is powerless to do more than choose the crime to be committed. This model has been named the "dilemma model" by William Bowen in his book *The Wage Price Issue.*

In the past I have accepted the basic logic of the dilemma model. However, in the last year I have come to believe that it is not an appropriate model for the United States. Its most important shortcoming, as I have hinted earlier, is its failure to give enough weight to effects on the nonunion sector, and particularly the failure to take into account the autonomous rise in wages in the nonunion sector resulting from the rise in productivity there.

Suppose that we have an economy in which, without unions or with ineffective ones, prices are stable and money wages are rising at an average annual rate of say 3 percent. Suppose further that strong unions are organized in half of this economy, selected so that its preunion rate of wage increase does not differ from the average, and that the effect of these unions is to raise the rate of increase of wages in their sector to 4 percent annually. Very probably the ultimate outcome of unionization would be to reduce the rate of growth of wages in the nonunion sector to 2 percent but to leave the average annual increase unaltered for the economy as a whole. If this is correct, the whole effect would be consistent with the national wage policy usually prescribed and would not call for either government intervention or union restraint to avoid inflation.

To be sure, the situation just envisaged raises prices in the union sector, and if there is downward price rigidity in the nonunion sector, it could, at least temporarily, raise some broad price indexes. However, the nonunion sectors of the economy are not those usually characterized by substantial price rigidity, so that the effect is likely to be almost entirely on the structure of relative prices and not on the absolute level of prices. In this formulation we do not need to consider downward wage rigidity in the nonunion sector, since the effect of the unions is not to put downward pressure on wages in this sector but only to reduce the rate at which these wages rise. This result relies on our assumption that when labor markets are not tight, most nonunion employers see no need to emulate union wage increases fully in order to hold their workers. I also assume that nonunion employers are under no immediate threat of organization by an aggressively expanding union movement.

The dynamic model just discussed need not involve any unemployment as a result of union wage pressures provided that employment is initially growing in both sectors. The higher relative prices of the products of the union sector will cause some decrease in the amounts of them demanded, and rising relative wages in the union sector will lead to faster substitution of capital for labor in this sector. Unless these effects are large, however, they will merely slow the growth of employment in the sector and not cause it to decline absolutely. Even if there is an absolute decline in employment in the union sector, the workers displaced could be absorbed in the nonunion sector, whose rate of growth will have increased. The unemployment created even in this case is frictional or structural rather than the kind resulting from a deficiency of aggregate demand. Indeed, it is precisely this increased supply of labor to the nonunion sector that enables it to slacken its rate of wage increase.

The situation created by different rates of growth of wages in the two sectors as a result solely of union pressures is not entirely a happy one. It would undoubtedly contribute to underemployment in the nonunion sector—to having too many people trapped in low-productivity activities like domestic service and marginal agriculture who should be absorbed into more productive activities. It is not impossible to imagine a national wage policy designed to cope with this kind of malallocation. But such a policy would be of a totally different kind than the policy generally proposed. It would have to address itself directly to the problem of relative wages, and not to the general level of wages.

My conclusion is that we do not need a national wage policy designed to govern the general level of wages. If unions need to exercise restraint in their wage bargaining, it is not so much to prevent inflation as to preserve employment for their members. The incentives for this kind of restraint are provided by employer resistance to union demands and by short hours or layoffs and not by admonitions from public officials to act in the national interest.

Let me make it as clear as I can that my opposition to a national wage policy is not based on opposition to any sort of macroeconomic policy for the federal government. The government, including the Federal Reserve System, has the very important and difficult obligation of maintaining a reasonably stable value of money and of assuring reasonably full employment. To develop policies that will assure a proper balance between these objectives in a changing economy subject to cyclical fluctuations is a continuing challenge. But if we can control aggregate demand so that there is neither a strong pressure of excess demand nor a large nor persistent unemployment of labor and other resources, there is no need for an additional and independent policy on the rate of increase of wages. Within the restraints provided by monetary and fiscal policy, the general level of wages can be left to the determination of employers and unions. The only further purpose to be served by a wage policy would be to decide the division of income between workers and others, and this in my view the government should not do.

Perhaps we need to pay less attention to the formulation of over-all national wage policies of the kind that cannot be implemented, and ask how the actual present labor policies of the federal government affect the wage determination process. The over-all policies set forth in the Economic Reports of the President call for wage restraint, but the actual impact of policy as it works in collective-bargaining situations is more likely to be on the side of wage increases. For example, we can ask whether the main pressure of fact-finding boards in emergency disputes has not been usually on employers to give larger increases to get a settlement rather than on unions to moderate their demands. Perhaps there are changes in the procedures of handling emergency disputes or in the criteria used by fact-finders that would help to eliminate any tendency for intervention to work toward higher pay for industries that are not short of labor and already have high wages. We can ask, too, whether it makes for better wage settlements to permit strikers to collect unemployment insurance while they are on strike (as is now possible in New York state and on the railroads), or for that matter, whether we should permit employers to carry strike-loss insurance or to enter into loss-sharing contracts. We can also ask whether the Walsh-Healy Act, on the rather infrequent occasions when it is effective, is not used to support high union wages by denying government contracts to nonunion employers, even though their employees may have chosen to remain non-union in an election conducted under the terms of other federal legislation. I do not mean to prejudge any of these issues; each might merit a long discussion in its own right, with much to be said on both sides. My only concern is to point out that the real national wage policy is made up of what the government does and not of what it says, and that the two are often at variance.

Perhaps the question of wage policy also suggests a lesson for economists. We often learn a great deal from the construction of formal theoretical models of the economy, and those whose talents lie in this direction should certainly be encouraged to expand and refine these models. It is dangerous in the extreme, however, to use these models as a guide to policy formation unless great care has been taken to assure that the assumptions of the models, both explicit and implicit, are consistent with the conditions of the problem for which policy is being made. In my judgment, the implications of formal models for wage changes are not yet sufficiently well worked out to form the basis of a national wage policy. For the time being at least I think that the process of wage determination as it has evolved in our political economy will come closer to taking account of all the relevant conditions and requirements than any formal scheme developed by economic science.

A Positive Wage Policy

WALTER P. REUTHER

Walter Reuther has been president of the United Automobile Workers since 1946. This statement on wage policy is taken from his report on economic conditions presented at the 1964 convention of the UAW.

We in the UAW have long recognized that in the long run, when the economy is in balance, improvements in real wages must be closely related to improvements in national productivity. Wage and fringe benefit gains must come out of the fruits of our advancing technology, and not out of the pockets of consumers through price increases.

But this principle assumes an economy already in balance. . . . When the economy is slack due to insufficiency of consumer demand and a drain-off of profits in excess of investment, a wage advance somewhat in excess of productivity is needed to help restore the balance. In the same way, if the economy were operating at full production, with an excess of demand over what production could supply, it might be desirable for the time being to increase wages somewhat less than the normal rise of productivity so as to reduce the pressures of consumer demand and make more funds available for investment.

There can be no question today either as to the existence of imbalance in our economy or as to its nature. For the past several years consumer demand has been shrinking as a proportion of our potential capacity to produce, and this lag has been a major cause of economic slack and rising unemployment. At the same time, retained profits and other internally generated funds have been piling up in corporate treasuries in excess of investment opportunities, even after payment of record-breaking dividends. The dividends go largely to wealthy families, for whom job-creating investment opportunities are also lacking. This is the serious imbalance in the economy which must be corrected before the principle of relating labor's economic gains to the rate of productivity advance can have any real validity. The immediate and urgent necessity is for a wage policy designed to correct the imbalance. For at least the short-run future, real wages, salaries and fringe benefits must increase faster than productivity until a workable balance between demand and capacity has been achieved.

Such wage and fringe benefit improvements, of course, must not be gained at the cost of price increases. That would defeat the whole purpose of enlarging consumer demand. They must come out of the swollen profits which represent the other side of the economic imbalance. . . .

A NEGATIVE POLICY IN THE PAST

We must reverse the negative wage policies which have dominated both business and government thinking in the past. Almost every discussion of wage policy has been centered on the fear of inflation or of difficulties in meeting trade competition from abroad, even though both dangers are greatly exaggerated and, to the extent that they exist, do not stem from wage levels at all. In consequence of these fears, however, the wage policies favored not only by business but by important voices in government have almost invariably been restrictive. The imagined threat has been that wage increases might be too large—never that they might be too small. Average wage increases which have fallen below even the levels dictated by these restrictive policies have been greeted with approval when their obvious deficiencies should have prompted a call for remedy.

Testifying before the Joint Economic Committee in July [1963], for example, Secretary of the Treasury Douglas Dillon said:

> Our success in holding costs and prices steady during the current expansion has been gratifying. Over recent years, the annual rate of wage increase in manufacturing has dropped steadily, and for the past two years has been slightly below the yearly gains in productivity.

The facts are true, but their recognition should not have been a source of self-satisfaction. It should have been marked by an expression of determination to correct the deficiency in the interest of the whole economy.

WAGES AND PRODUCTIVITY SINCE 1956

Secretary Dillon's statement grossly understates the lag between workers' buying power and productivity, because he compares dollar wages, without any adjustment for price changes, and physical productivity, which does take price changes into account. The fact is that, not just in the past two years, but ever since 1956, workers' buying power has been lagging behind even the retarded rate of productivity advance resulting from failure to make full use of our productive capacity, and the lag has not been slight, but very substantial.

Between 1956 and 1963, average straight-time hourly earnings of manufacturing production workers increased by 25.4 per cent, but over half of this was eroded by a 12.7 per cent rise in the cost of living, so that the buying power of an hour's pay ("real" wages) rose by only 11.3 per cent, an average of only 1.5 per cent per year. During this same period, in spite of the depressing effects of economic stagnation over the greater part of it, aggravated by two recessions, the amount of goods and services produced in return for an average hour's pay in the private economy increased by 24.4 percent, an average of 3.2 per cent a year—over twice as fast as real wages.

In the past two years the gap has widened at an even faster rate. As Mr. Dillon pointed out, even actual dollar wages (straight-time hourly earnings in manufacturing), without any adjustment for cost-of-living increase, rose more slowly than productivity. When the cost-of-living adjustment is made, real wages are found to have increased from 1961 to 1963 at an average rate of only 1.4 per cent, while the average annual productivity increase, at 3.7 per cent, was over 2½ times as great.

These earnings figures apply only to manufacturing production workers, and do not include either the pay of salaried workers or the cost of fringe benefits for both groups. From data in the 1964 report of the Council of Economic Advisers, it is possible to estimate the increase in total real compensation per manhour of all employes in manufacturing, which does include fringe benefits and employer contributions to social insurance. Here the lag behind productivity is somewhat smaller, but it is still substantial.

Real compensation per manhour paid of all employes in manu-

Real Employee Compensation and Productivity per Manhour,[a] 1956-1963

Year	Productivity (output per manhour) in the private economy	Real employe compensation per manhour in manufacturing	Private economy
	(1956 = 100)		
1956	100.0	100.0	100.0
1957	103.5	102.5	102.4
1958	106.1	103.5	103.2
1959	109.9	106.9	107.2
1960	112.0	109.4	109.4
1961	115.8	111.2	111.8
1962	120.2	114.0	114.8
1963	124.4	116.8	117.0

[a] All three indexes are based on hours *paid.*

SOURCE: Computed from data of Council of Economic Advisers and Bureau of Labor Statistics.

facturing increased by only 16.8 per cent from 1956 to 1963, an average increase of only 2.2 per cent per year, scarcely two-thirds as fast as the average productivity advance of 3.2 per cent a year.

Nor is this situation confined to manufacturing workers. Over the same period, real compensation of all employes in the private economy (excluding government for which productivity cannot be measured) increased by only 17.0 per cent, or an average of 2.3 per cent a year. By 1963, the real compensation of such employes would have had to be 6.3 per cent greater than it was in order to have matched the rate of productivity advance since 1956. Since employe compensation in 1963 totaled $340 billion, an increase of 6.3 per cent would have injected an additional $21 billion of purchasing power into the economy, almost twice as much as the tax cut, and would have gone a long way toward making up the deficiency in demand. . . .

ACCELERATING PRODUCTIVITY

The rate of productivity advance to which wage and salary increases must be geared should not be that for any arbitrarily-chosen short period of years, but should be the trend revealed by analysis of experience over a long period of years. Any such analysis, however, must take into account the fact that productivity is not just an advancing force in which each year the rate of productivity tends to be higher than the year before; it is an accelerating force in which the rate of advance tends to be more and more rapid as the years pass and one technological breakthrough follows on another.

Analysis of productivity data extending back over more than half a century establishes beyond any reasonable doubt the fact that there has been a persistent accelerating trend in the rate of productivity advance—moving forward from a rate of one percent or less per year at the beginning of the period, in 1909, to a "normal" of approximately 4 percent per year today.

ADJUSTMENTS FOR PRICE CHANGES

A positive and constructive wage policy must also be based on the facts as to real wages, after adjustment for price increases. It must not repeat Secretary Dillon's error in comparing wage increases and productivity without taking cost-of-living changes into account. To base wage policy on such comparisons would mean that workers would be expected to accept a reduced share in the total product of their work every time the cost of living increases. In some years, when the cost of living has gone up faster than the rate of productivity advance, such a policy would have meant that the average worker's standard of living would actually have fallen, even though his productivity had increased. Productivity is invariably measured in the equivalent of physical terms—not the dollar value of an hour's output, but the physical volume, arrived at by adjusting the dollar value by any change in the selling price per unit. Thus, to be comparable, wages must be adjusted by any change in their buying power, as measured by the Consumer Price Index.

Although it has at times fallen into the same error as Secretary Dillon, the Council of Economic Advisers in its 1964 report clearly established the proper method of comparing wages with productivity, when it said:

> It is a matter of arithmetic that labor's share in total income will remain unchanged if total hourly labor compensation rises in the same proportion as labor productivity when prices are constant.

It clearly follows that if prices are not constant, then account must be taken of the price change, for the same arithmetic mentioned by the Council shows that labor's share in total income will fall if total hourly compensation rises only in the same proportion as labor productivity when prices are rising.

This, of course, is the principle behind the combination of annual improvement factor and cost-of-living escalator wage adjustments which has for many years been in effect between the UAW and companies in the auto industry and other industries. The improvement factor increases are related in principle, though not adequately in practice, to the long-term rate of productivity advance in the economy, while the cost-of-living clause provides for additional adjustments in wages in accordance with changes in the Consumer Price Index.

PRICE-PROFIT POLICIES

In industries in which a higher-than-average rate of productivity advance is combined with substantial power to administer prices, abuse of that power by employers for the purpose of obtaining excessive profits can create a condition in which the principle of gearing wage increases only to the national rate of productivity advance is no longer valid. The holy theory behind the use of national productivity advance as a yardstick is that the fruits of productivity should be equitably shared—not just between employers and workers, but among employers, workers and consumers. The Council of Economic Advisers made that perfectly clear when it proposed its price-wage guideposts. In its 1964 Report, for example, it said:

> The general guidepost for prices specifies that when an industry's trend productivity is growing less rapidly than the national trend, prices can appropriately rise enough to accommodate the labor cost increases indicated by the general wage guidepost. Similarly, in an industry whose trend productivity is growing more rapidly than the national average, product prices should be lowered enough to distribute to the industry's customers the labor-cost savings it would make under the general wage guidepost.

The solution urged by the Council is for high-productivity firms to make price cuts. But it was compelled to admit that "It is fair to say that large industrial enterprises thus far have not widely heeded this advice."

Interestingly enough, this advice has been followed in Great

Britain by a subsidiary of a U.S. corporation that has stubbornly refused to reduce excessive prices here. The *Christian Science Monitor* of Feb. 5, 1964, reported that Ford of Britain had cut prices of its smallest car, the Anglia, by amounts ranging, in U. S. equivalents, from $67 to $101, in spite of the fact that it had just granted a five per cent wage increase. The *Monitor* reported:

> Ford, however, can cut its prices because of extremely high production and considerable increases in productivity. It can do so in spite of having granted a 5 per cent wage increase.

The pay increase itself was made in spite of restrictive wage policies of the British government. The report stated:

> At the same time it was made, this wage award was strongly criticized. It was held responsible to some extent for a subsequent general repudiation of the government's "guiding light" for pay rises (between 3 and 3.5 percent).

The *Monitor* noted that:

> The Ford move seems to ask: If increased productivity leads to price cuts, to record output and soaring profits, how can it be wrong to reward it? If it is not specially rewarded, how can its continuance be expected?

These questions might well find an echo in the head offices of Ford and its fellow auto makers in the United States.

PRODUCTIVITY AND PROFITS IN THE AUTO INDUSTRY

The automobile industry is one in which a rate of productivity advance much above the national average is associated with profits in the major firms which are also far above the national average when measured as a rate of return on investment. The record-breaking profits of the leading companies in the past two years are discussed in the section of this report dealing with the automobile industry.

The industry has also had a very high rate of productivity advance for a great many years. Before World War II, studies made by the Bureau of Labor Statistics (BLS) found auto industry productivity to be advancing much faster than the average for all manufacturing. BLS, however, has published no auto industry productivity figures since 1940.

The Federal Reserve Board does compute a production index for the auto industry, including the parts and accessories manufacturers, which makes it possible to approximate the extent of productivity advance in the industry in the postwar period.

The data now available show that, from 1947 through 1963, the production of the auto industry more than doubled, increasing by 110.1 per cent. During the same period, according to BLS data, the number of production worker manhours paid in the industry declined by 1.9 per cent. This means that the industry's productivity per manhour paid increased by 114.2 per cent—an average of 4.9 per cent per year over the entire period.

This compares with a productivity advance in the whole private economy for the same period of 64.7 per cent—an average of only 3.2 per cent per year.

The industry has at times contended that the use of 1947 as a base year is unsound because postwar conversion problems in 1947 depressed productivity in that year. However, if the postwar period is split into two halves, from 1947 to 1955 and from 1955 to 1963, the average annual rate of productivity advance in each half is found to be the same 4.9 per cent. . . .

The auto industry's higher-than-average rate of productivity advance, combined with its fabulous high profits, means that it could well afford to cut prices substantially while still granting generous wage increases. The industry has shown no intention, however, of cutting prices by any significant amount . . .

Evidence that substantial wage increases could be paid out of profits is provided by a U. S. Department of Commerce survey, which shows that a combination of rising productivity, lagging real wages and higher prices have been responsible for the record-breaking profits of 1963.[1] . . .

THE INFLATION ARGUMENT

Substantial wage increases and fringe benefit improvements now, sufficient to help bring consumer demand into balance with productive capacity, would strengthen the economy without threatening inflation. They could not force prices up by causing demand for goods and services to exceed our capacity to produce them, because it is the excessive slack in demand that makes

1. *Survey of Current Business*, November 1963.

them necessary. They need not force prices up through cost increases, because the record-breaking profits earned by major corporations in 1962 and 1963 testify to the ability of these corporations to absorb increases in hourly labor costs without any increase in prices.

Those who favor a restrictive wage policy argue that wage increases make our products less competitive in world markets and so increase our balance of payments difficulties. It should be noted that these arguments fail to take into account the fact that our balance of payments problems arise from quite other causes than trade deficits. For nearly 70 years, in every year since 1894, we have been able to sell in the markets of the world more than we purchased. Our sales of finished manufactures, which have a high labor content, have been double our imports of similar products in recent years.

Do the Government's Guidelines Really Guide?

R. HEATH LARRY

R. Heath Larry has been administrative vice president for labor relations of the United States Steel Corporation since 1958. These comments on the applicability of the Council's "guideposts" to the steel industry appeared in Personnel *in the winter of 1962.*

As an anonymous wit once observed, the younger and the older generations have all the answers, while the generation in between is stuck with all the questions. I suspect that those government officials who are now seeking new ways to insure that collective bargaining better serves the national interest most often feel like the inbetween generation—stuck with all the questions, while management and labor sound as if they have all the answers.

To be sure, though their reasons may differ, both industrial and labor leaders show substantial agreement in their opposition to government policies that they believe infringe on their rightful areas of freedom.

Certainly, if "eternal vigilance is the price of freedom," it cannot be entirely unhealthy that the first reaction of both labor and management to the appearance of government in new roles should be that of the mother who called out, "Junior, go see what your little brother is doing—and tell him to stop it."

On the other hand, it would hardly be healthy, either, were we always ready to oppose, but unwilling to be informed; sure of what we are against, but unsure of what we are for. In the present running debate, it behooves us, therefore, to be constructive as well as critical.

With this aim in view, let's first consider what led to the Administration's efforts to improve the impact of collective bargaining from the standpoint of the national interest; then let's consider the meaning of what it has done; and, finally, let's explore the possibility of more useful alternative courses.

The outstanding background fact is, of course, that the Forties and Fifties were decades of continuous inflation. The effects of wars and semi-wars and of monetary and fiscal policy were partly to blame, but another key reason was the unchanging pattern of wage increases that far outran the increases in productivity however these were calculated. Moreover, the market was less and less able to sustain the translation of this rising cost pattern into higher prices.

Industry's efforts to resist this pattern of increasing employment costs were all too often lumped with union efforts to maintain the pattern simply as a "hardening of the attitudes" on both sides. But the economic vise finally tightened to the point where competitive survival became the nation's problem, not just industry's. The competitive place of American industry in world markets was inseparable from the problems of gold balances, balance of payments, international trade, and national defense. Thus the public and the government could no longer dismiss the industry-labor struggle over employment costs with, "A plague on both your houses."

It was becoming clear that continuing inflation was hampering both the nation's growth and all attempts to achieve full employment. It was becoming clear, too, that continuing inflation—which in effect purloined from the future to create the appearance of affluence in the present—was no more sound in the long run for Uncle Sam than it was for the individual. And it was also becoming clear that even if the increases in employment costs were not the sole offender, inflation could not be curbed—the competitive position of American industry could not be improved—unless unions in collective bargaining gave at least fair recognition to the rate of productivity growth.

No longer was it true that in collective bargaining peace, alone, was of ultimate importance. Industrial productivity was now even more important. The result was a spate of "helpful" suggestions intended to bring collective bargaining in line with the national interest, such as inviting participation by representatives of the "public," summit meetings, special legislation, and, finally, the "guideline" approach. It is this last remedy that I propose to discuss.

As a point of departure, let me quote from a speech the then Secretary of Labor, Arthur Goldberg, made in Chicago in February 1962:

> I think that the Government should do more statistical and economic analyses so that the people can be advised of the relevant facts before

they settle, and not after. . . . I think the Government has an obligation to define the national interest and assert it when it reaches important proportions in any area of our economy. And I would like to state this is what your Government is going to do. It is going to unhesitatingly assert and define the national interest because, after all, we regard this to be our obligation to all the people.

Now, presumably, the official "definition" of the national interest, as it relates to wage and price policy, was the one set forth in the Committee of Economic Advisers' Report attached to the President's Economic Report of January 1962. In the chapter, "Guideposts for Noninflationary Wage and Price Behavior,"[1] there is, first, a declaration of the public interest in wage and price decisions that affect the whole economy, followed by the suggestion that "an informed public, aware of the significance of major wage bargains and price decisions, and equipped to judge for itself their compatibility with the national interest, can help create an atmosphere in which the parties to such decisions will exercise their powers responsibly."

This concept of encouraging voluntary responses, together with the acknowledgment that there are no simple tests, that figures on national productivity might be debatable, and that there are many qualifications to "general guides," all made the report seem, on the whole, a worthwhile contribution to the problem.

Certainly, it contributed some much-needed emphasis in many ways. On the plus side, for example:

1. It offers an admirable exposition of why inflation is harmful and should be overcome.
2. It makes clear that if employment costs rise at a higher rate than the rate of the rise in productivity, sooner or later prices will have to rise and inflation will continue.
3. It confirms that only as productive efficiency increases can there be any increase in "real" income as distinct from "money" wages.
4. It acknowledges that market forces are the desirable discipline of prices, and shows how in some periods when money wages were rising slowly there were actually greater rises in real income than in periods when wages were rising more rapidly.
5. It also acknowledges that overall price stability, which is attainable if employment costs remain within productivity trends, "should be achieved in a manner consistent with the

1. [Reprinted on pp. 88–94 in this volume. *Editor.*]

flexible response of individual prices and wage rates to changes in cost and demand within an environment of dynamic competition."

6. It recognizes the problems of measuring productivity, and indicates that there is still much to learn about them.
7. It points out that its productivity guidelines are neither "rules" nor "mechanical formulas" for determining whether a particular price or wage decision is inflationary.
8. It advocates, in general, that in making their agreements the parties involved voluntarily assume responsibility to an enlightened public opinion.

These points made by the report are all to the good. On the other side of the ledger, though, are several disturbing features:

1. While stressing that "it is undesirable that [labor and management] should bargain implicitly about the general price level," the report also recommends that "it is desirable that [they] bargain explicitly about the distribution of income of the particular firms or industries." Now wholly aside from the debatable question of the desirability of bargaining about the sharing of receipts, surely any bargaining about the "distribution of income" necessarily involves implicit or explicit bargaining about the price level in the firm or industry in question. So here we must ask: Doesn't bargaining between employers and a union, even where there is only an implicit assumption or understanding about price stability or price levels, raise serious antitrust problems? The whole guideline concept is undoubtedly most troublesome on this score.

2. While the report does acknowledge the problems involved in measuring productivity trends, it sets forth tables of increases in output per man-hour only, and equates these increases with increases in productivity. But, even though we still have much to learn about measuring all the factors contributing to productivity, it is generally agreed that calculations based simply on output per man-hour show increases in productivity to be greater than they really are. The use of figures embodying a national tendency toward overstatement is certainly a questionable "assist" to the national interest.

3. While generally arguing for restraint in union demands, at least in the context of the wage patterns of the past 20 years, the report nevertheless seems to show a strong bias in favor of labor. It puts great emphasis on the desirability of "price stability"; yet

it suggests that "average money wages should follow a generally rising pattern," and that, as a general guide, "the rate of increase in wage rates (including fringe benefits) in cash industry *be equal to* (it doesn't say "should not exceed") the trend rate of over-all productivity increase."

Yet in the past 10 to 15 years profits have declined so markedly as a share of the national income while the share of wages has risen that there is great concern whether sufficient profit incentive remains to attract capital into job-producing opportunities. If the guideline approach is used to accomplish some kind of price freeze, while leaving the wage line flexible, the whole approach will have been a destructive blow to our free-market economy.

4. Though the Government's aim is to encourage growth, increase employment, and improve our trade position in the world market, the report does not seem to consider the broader potential of a different kind of restraint:

Since it sees no serious defect in the market system as a discipline for prices and profits, the report surely might have at least considered whether just as much increase in *real* employee income lies in an alternative policy of wage rate changes substantially below the productivity trend rates and even periods of no change at all. This policy would be a much stronger encouragement to new market penetration—and hence more employment—than the policy presented in the report. One can only guess, but this may be a reflection of political bias.

Now we come to the difficulties of translating the guidelines into action.

First, they tend to have greater impact in highly visible, well-publicized bargaining situations than in smaller, more obscure ones. In local bargaining, many unions, especially those not well known to the public, seem to pay little attention to the guidelines—and get away with it.

Second, many unions use the highest figures in the report's productivity tables as a springboard for their bargaining, contending that the meaning of the report is that their wages should rise *at least* that much.

And, third, since publication of the CEA's report, the government's manner of "assertion" seems to have put another light on the entire "definition" effort.

As the well-known labor reporter A. H. Raskin has pointed out in discussing this subject:

The question is whether the CEA [is] not itself the victim of an inherent contradiction in believing that the economy could at once be controlled and uncontrolled. Once rules are laid down for voluntary restraint, the danger is that they will have to be enforced.[2]

This is, of course, an inherent danger of "definition" by government, as distinct from definition by the accumulative thinking and writings of academicians, economists, and the like—even though at first blush it seems reasonable that if anyone is going to define the national interest, it should be a government spokesman.

If the process of "assertion" is going to go along with the process of "definition" (whether it should do so is, of course, a separate problem), the "definition" should be made considerably more precise and understandable, or the line will confuse more than it guides.

Here is a case in point: Had you been in the steel business what would you have expected to happen last April [3] in the light of these guideline statements in the report?

1. Over-all price stability, the report noted, did not require that all prices be stable. Relative price changes were the "signals and stimuli which foster the efficiency and guide the growth of" the economy.

2. "It is quite true, of course," the report observed, "that when employment costs per man-hour rise more rapidly than output per man-hour, prices sooner or later will increase."

3. After noting the absence of price increases in steel since 1958, as well as the fact that the 1956 and 1959 agreements with the Steelworkers had raised employment costs about 8 percent and 3.7 percent respectively, the report conceded that these increases were "above the overall trend of productivity increase."

4. Over-all stability, the report went on, should be "achieved in a manner consistent with the flexible response of individual prices and wage rates to changes in cost and demand within an environment of dynamic competition."

2. "Mr. Kennedy's Guidelines—Are They Drawn Too Tight?" *The Reporter*, June 21, 1962, p. 19.

3. [On April 10, 1962, the United States Steel Corporation announced the $6 per ton price increase which precipitated the well-known attack by President Kennedy. On April 13, U.S. Steel rescinded its announced increase, and shortly thereafter the five companies that had followed its lead in raising prices took the same action. One year later, in April 1963, smaller across-the-board increases were announced by the corporations. *Editor*.]

5. Shortly thereafter we learn that "productivity is a guide rather than a rule" and "the pattern of wages and prices among industries is and should be responsive to forces other than changes in productivity."

6. Then comes the statement: "Price stability within any particular industry is not necessarily a correct guide to price and wage decisions in that industry."

7. On the following page is a mixture of clues. First, the report states that the "general guide . . . is that the rate of increase . . . in each industry be equal to the trend rate of over-all productivity increase." Prices reductions are called for if an industry's productivity exceeds the over-all rate. On the other hand, an appropriate increase in prices is called for "if the *opposite relationship* prevails." But when does this "opposite relationship" prevail?

Further, we find the suggestion that wage rates should "fall short of the general guide" in an industry that is hard pressed to provide full employment for its workforce, or where the wage rates are high in comparison with other industry rates, as the result of a strong bargaining position of the workers.

These two conditions sound as though they refer to an industry like steel. Since the steel settlement represented an employment-cost increase of about 2.5 percent, did this "fall short" so that the "opposite relationship" could not be said to prevail?

Let us remember here that nowhere in the report is there a precise statement of what the over-all trend rate is. One table shows that annual increases in productivity for the total private economy for the period 1909-1960 were 2.4 percent; and for the period 1954 to 1960, 2.6 percent. But you can also find figures of 3.0 percent and 3.5 percent, depending on where you look.

Let us also remember the comment that steel employment costs had been exceeding the guide trend, and remember also that those in the industry had maintained all along that even output per man-hour was not rising in steel by as much as 2 percent.

What, then, did all this mean to the steel industry?

The plain fact is that the steel negotiators did not know whether they were, or were not, at or within the "general guide." As between the companies involved and the union there were no price assumptions whatever; they considered neither price stability nor price increases, nor decreases. . . .

No reasonable person urges a tight system of wage and price

controls in peacetime, but if "assertion" there must be, then "definition" there must also be with more "micro-economic accuracy," if even the wary are not to be tripped up by what are supposed to be guidelines.

I don't know whether our reasons are the same, but I agree with Dr. George W. Taylor that "experience with the initial attempt at using general guides to define and assert the public interest in private wage determination already indicates a need to rethink the problem."

How, then, shall we rethink it? First of all, we should remember that our economy's greatest source of strength is its basis on the concept of a free society, and its system of free markets and free enterprise. Free collective bargaining is a part of that picture, too.

Presidential adviser Paul Samuelson has said that the pricing process in the United States is "so complex that the whole nature of our economic system would have to be different once we decided not to rely on market forces." But some changes have already been in the making—and one of the root causes has been that labor costs have become so little responsive to market forces. Why, otherwise, the need for the "restraints" of the guidelines? More important, how can we bring about a change in the basic forces that have created the problem?

I strongly believe that unless there is a reorientation of the bargaining framework more in line with the employer's competitive market situation, our free-market economy will ultimately give way to a controlled economy, because it will be unable to measure up in world competition. And it would be tragic for a so-called free economy to be blamed for failures that came about only because it was not in truth free.

I suggest that there is a pressing need for labor and management to learn how to cooperate in pursuit of a different kind of guideline for judging the desirability of future changes in employment costs. The new guideline for assessing the merits of any proposed change should be simply: It is likely to contribute to an increase in employment? Perhaps we should call this not a guideline, but simply an objective.

This may sound naïve and even misdirected. But I think it is a sound assumption that if employment in any enterprise grows, it will be because the employer has found it possible and profitable to expand his market. If employment grows, there will have been capital growth beforehand and improvement of the American position in world trade.

The pursuit of this objective does not mean following the discredited purchasing-power theory; it does not mean operating the economy on the basis of federally accumulated statistics; it does not mean, on the one hand, automatic annual increases, as the Administration's guideline can be interpreted to advocate, nor, on the other, does it necessarily mean denial of any increases at all at any time for any employee.

But it does mean attempting to form a judgment as to whether the nature or magnitude of a wage or benefit proposal will tend to restrict employment in that unit or to encourage it.

Government, academicians, employers, and union leaders would, of course, have to understand and make clear to the public and to employees that in a free economy jobs cannot be either preserved or brought into existence by legislative or bargaining *fiat;* that no job can exist for long unless there is sufficient profit incentive for its being; that every cost increase has some effect, sooner or later, on price and employment, and that employment-cost increases in a company or industry whose market is not expanding cannot help but tend to depress employment opportunities.

Raising the cost of labor cannot of itself lead to more employment of labor; its tendency may be precisely in the opposite direction. If, as Gompers used to say, labor's objective must always be "more," let it set its sights on what it takes to get "more" employment. This must be made an alternative to simply "more" in the pay envelope. Employers have a heavy burden of communication here, but I feel it would no longer be resented as it once was. Today's labor leaders want to do what is good for the country—and even for the employer—though at times it may take a good deal of sophistication to make it politically palatable. There are increasing signs of labor's cooperative attitude in the labor-costs-*vs.*-profits situation, but too often the cooperation is withheld until the employer's back is flat against the wall. We must find ways to achieve cooperation before these problems become crises. Failure to do so can mean that our free-market society will wither—a prospect with no gains for anyone.

Automation, Jobs, and Manpower

CHARLES C. KILLINGSWORTH

Charles Killingsworth is professor of industrial relations at Michigan State University. His statement before the Senate Subcommittee on Employment and Manpower (from which this selection is taken) has been very influential on the "pro-structural" side of the structural unemployment controversy.

AUTOMATION, ESPECIALLY IN its advanced forms, fundamentally changes the man-machine relation. Such a change is not unprecedented in economic history. The assembly line, as it replaced earlier techniques, helped to create literally millions of simple, repetitive jobs that could be learned in a few hours or a few days. Anybody who had two hands, two eyes, and a capacity to endure monotony could do the work.

Today we have the electric eye, the iron hand, the tin ear, and the electronic brain. We also have the know-how to tie them together in self-regulating systems that can perform an enormous variety of jobs. There are two major results. One is a great reduction in the number of simple, repetitive jobs where all you need is your five senses and an untrained mind. The other result is a great increase in the number of jobs involved in designing, engineering, programing, and administering these automatic production systems. Industry needs many more scientists, engineers, mathematicians, and other highly trained people, and many fewer blue-collar workers. . . .

Between 1957 and 1962 in manufacturing, production workers declined by nearly a million, while nonproduction workers increased by about a third of a million. The net change was a reduction of about 600,000 in employment.

Not all of the increase in white-collar employment in manufacturing was due to automation, of course, and not all of the newly hired employees were scientists and engineers. But the changing composition of employment was partly due to automation. Moreover, what happened from 1957 to 1962 was the continuation of a postwar trend. Chart 1 shows what has happened to the ratio

CHART 1. *The Ratio of Nonproduction Employment in Manufacturing, 1919 to mid-1963*

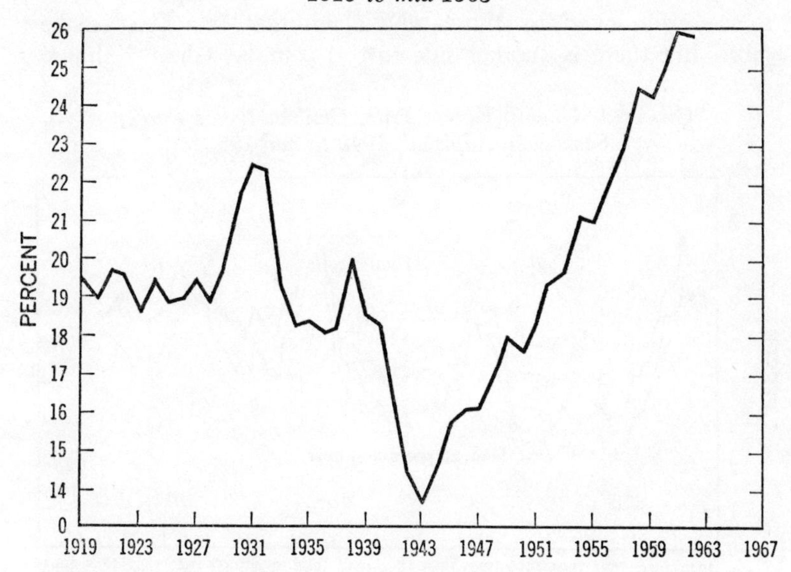

SOURCE: Adapted from U.S. Department of Labor, Bureau of Labor Statistics.

between production and nonproduction workers in manufacturing since 1919. Throughout the 1920s, the ratio fluctuated between narrow limits at around 19 or 20 percent. The Great Depression and World War II temporarily affected the ratio; at the outset of the depression, the blue-collar workers were laid off before the white-collar workers were, and in the war salesmen and clerks were drafted while blue-collar workers were added. By about 1951, the prewar ratio of about 1 white-collar worker to 4 blue-collar workers had been reestablished. But as automation gathered momentum during the 1950s, the ratio continued to change. It is now at about 26 percent and the trend is still strongly upward. Generally, the most highly automated industries have the highest ratio of white-collar workers. In chemicals and petroleum, for example, the ratio is 40 percent.

In an economy in which so many patterns are changing rapidly, broad averages and grand totals may conceal more than they reveal. I think that this is especially true of the effects of automation and the concomitant changes of today. Let us take as an example the figures showing total civilian employment since 1949. These figures . . . reveal the persistent upward trend in total employment—from 58 million jobs in 1949 to more than 68 million in 1963. This great increase is another piece of evidence often cited by those who claim that "machines make jobs." But there is another side to this coin. As Chart 2 shows,

CHART 2. *Unemployment Rate, Civilian Labor Force, Seasonally Adjusted, 1949 to mid-1963*

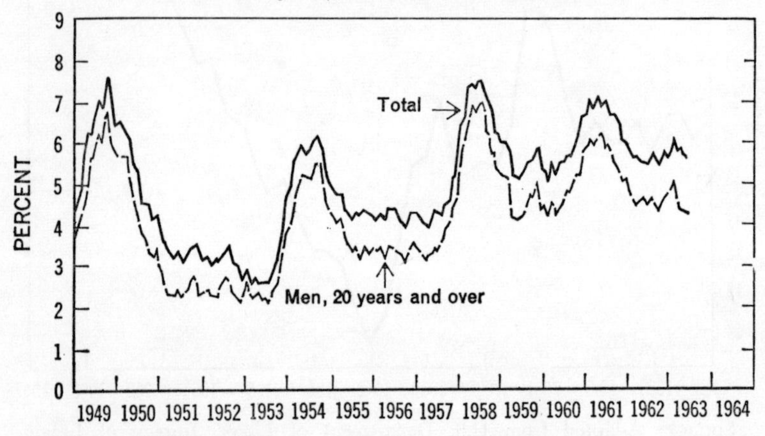

SOURCE: *Monthly Report of the Labor Force*, July 1963.
Data adjusted to new definitions adopted in January 1957. Beginning January 1960, data include Alaska and Hawaii.

unemployment crept upward during the latter part of this period —first two notches up, then one notch down, and then another two notches up. In 1951–1953, the average was about a 3-percent rate of unemployment. In 1962–1963, the average has been almost double that, or between 5½ and 6 percent.

It is not self-evident from these figures that any part of this creeping unemployment problem is due to automation or other basic changes in the patterns of the economy. There is eminent authority to the contrary. The President's Council of Economic Advisers [CEA] has repeatedly declared that automation and "structural unemployment" are not responsible for the gradual creep of unemployment about the 4-percent level of 1957. For example, the 1963 report of the Council includes the following passage:

> The problems of structural unemployment—of imperfect adaptation of jobs and workers—are persistent and serious, and they are thrown

into bold relief by the prolonged lack of sufficient job opportunities over the past 5 years. *But these problems of adaptation have not constituted a greater cause of unemployment in recent years than in earlier periods.* The source of the high unemployment rates in recent years, even in periods of cyclical expansion, lies not in labor market imbalance, but in the markets for goods and services. [Emphasis not in original.]

This analysis of the unemployment problem—that it is caused primarily by a lagging growth rate—is the basis for the administration's emphasis on a large tax cut as the top-priority item in the program to "get the economy moving again." Chairman Walter Heller of the CEA has repeatedly said that there is a "good prospect" that the tax cut would reduce unemployment to the 4-percent level.[1]

I think that it can be demonstrated that the Council is the victim of a half-truth. The lagging growth rate is only a part of the problem, and it may not be the most important part. I think that it is extremely unlikely that the proposed tax cut, desirable though it is as a part of a program, will prove to be sufficient to reduce unemployment to the 4-percent level. Perhaps it is true that in politics you can't get everything all at once. But I feel compelled to say that my analysis leads me to the conclusion that the administration's economic program is seriously incomplete. It gives woefully inadequate attention to what I regard as a key aspect of the unemployment problem of the 1960s; namely, labor market imbalance.

The Council's position on labor market imbalance, quoted above, rests on meticulous and extensive statistical studies. I am sure that the members of the Council, who are scholars of the highest competence and integrity, are willing to go where the facts lead them. The trouble is that their staff studies have not analyzed the figures which, in my judgment, clearly show a growing problem of labor market imbalance.

Let me preface my own analysis of those figures with a brief restatement of my argument to this point. The fundamental effect of automation on the labor market is to "twist" the pattern of demand—that is, it pushes down the demand for workers with little training while pushing up the demand for workers with large amounts of training.

1. [The Administration's tax-cut bill was passed by Congress in April 1964. *Editor.*]

The shift from goods to services is a second major factor which twists the labor market in the same way. There are some low-skilled, blue-collar jobs in service-producing industries; but the most rapidly growing parts of the service sector are health care and education, both of which require a heavy preponderance of highly trained people.

I have already presented some figures showing the changing patterns of demand for labor. These changing patterns of demand would not create labor market imbalance, however, unless changes in the supply of labor lagged behind. We turn now to the figures which show that such a lag has in fact developed.

Table 1 shows the relationship between rates of unemployment and levels of education of males 18 and over in two years —1950 and 1962.

TABLE 1. *Education and Unemployment, April 1950 and March 1962 (males, 18 and over)*

Years of school completed	Unemployment rates 1950	Unemployment rates 1962	Percentage change, 1950 to 1962
0 to 7	8.4	9.2	+9.5
8	6.6	7.5	+13.6
9 to 11	6.9	7.8	+13.0
12	4.6	4.8	+4.3
13 to 15	4.1	4.0	−2.4
16 or more	2.2	1.4	−36.4
All groups	6.2	6.0	−3.2

SOURCES: See appendix Tables A1, A2, A3 [in original article].

The overall unemployment rate was substantially the same in both years—6.2 in 1950 and 6.0 in 1962. But there was a redistribution of unemployment between these 2 years. The unemployment rates at the top of the educational attainment ladder went down, while the rates at the middle and lower rungs of the ladder went up substantially. The most significant figure in this table, I think, is the one showing the very large decrease in the unemployment rate of college graduates.

In a sense, these unemployment figures are only the part of the iceberg that is above the water. For a better understanding of their significance, we must consider also the changes in demand and supply that took place at the various educational levels

CHART 3. *The Changing Structure of Labor Force, Employment, and Unemployment, 1950–1962 (males, 18 and over)*

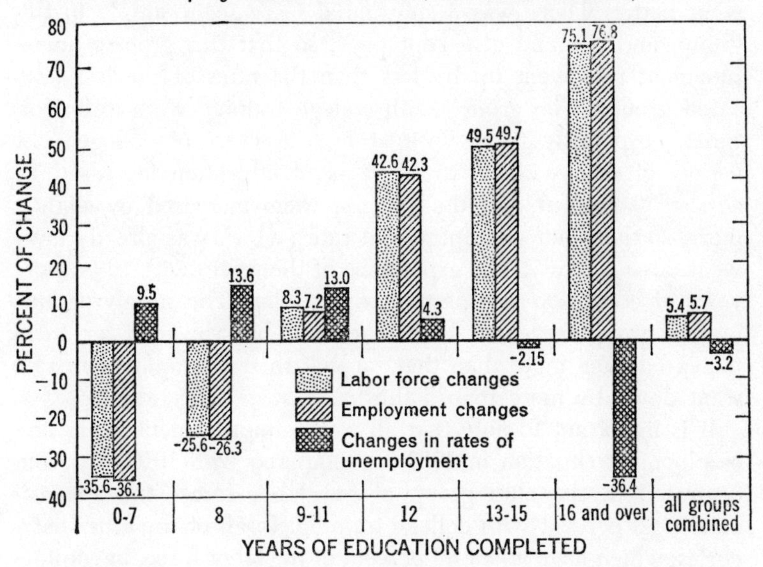

between 1950 and 1962. Chart 3 shows (for males 18 and over) the percentage changes in the supply of labor (labor force), in the demand for labor (employment), and in unemployment rates at various levels of educational attainment between 1950 and 1962. The left-hand bars show labor force changes, the center bars show employment changes, and the right-hand bars show unemployment rate changes. . . . The three bars at the far right of the chart show these changes for all groups combined; these aggregates obviously conceal some differences between educational levels which are of cardinal importance.

The bars for the 0 to 7 years of education group show that the number of this group in the labor force declined very greatly from 1950 to 1962; but the jobs held by this group declined even more, so that its unemployment rate went up. The supply of labor with 8 years of education also decreased, and the demand for this group decreased even more, and its unemployment rate increased by more than the increase in rate for the 0 to 7 classification. We see a different relationship between supply and demand in the 9 to 11 years of education group. Supply increased; demand also increased, but by less than the increase in supply, so that a higher unemployment rate resulted here too. The high-school graduates (12 years of education) fared somewhat better. There was a substantial increase in supply in this group, and demand also kept pace, so that this group's unemployment rate went up by less than the rates of the less educated groups. The groups with college training were quite fortunate, especially those with at least 4 years of college. The supply of men with 13 to 15 years of education increased by almost 50 percent, but the jobs for them increased by slightly more, so that their unemployment rate (which was already low) went down slightly. The experience of the group with 16 or more years of education was particularly striking. The supply of men in this group increased by 75 percent, but the jobs for them increased even more than that, so that their unemployment rate went down by more than a third.

It is important to note that all of the improvement in the unemployment situation in 1962, as compared with 1950, was concentrated in the elite group of our labor force—the approximately 20 percent with college training. In all of the other categories, which have about 80 percent of the labor force, unemployment rates were substantially higher in 1962 than in 1950. These figures, I contend, substantiate the thesis that the patterns of demand for labor have been twisted faster than the patterns of supply have changed, and that as a result we had a substantially greater degree of labor market imbalance in 1962 than in 1950.

But these figures do not fully reveal the power of the labor market twist. The "labor force" enumeration includes (with minor exceptions) only those who say that they have jobs or that they have actively sought work in the week preceding the survey. Those who have been out of work so long that they have given up hope and are no longer "actively seeking" work—but who would take a job if one were available—are simply not counted either as unemployed or as a member of the labor force. The percentage of a given category of the total population that is "in the labor force" (under the foregoing definition) is expressed as the "labor force participation rate." It seems probable that worsening employment prospects for a particular group over a long period would force down the labor force participation rate—*i.e.*, would squeeze a number of people out of the labor market altogether, in the sense that they would give up the continuing, active search for jobs. Conversely, it seems probable that improving employment prospects would tend to pull more people into the labor market and thus to raise the labor force participation rate. These two trends are indeed observable since 1950. The squeezing out of people at the lower end of the educational ladder and the pulling in of people at the upper end is another manifestation of the labor market twist. Table 2 presents the pertinent figures for males.

TABLE 2. *Labor Force Participation Rates and Educational Attainment, April 1950 and March 1962 (males, 18 and over)*

Years of school completed	Labor force participation rates		Percentage change,
	1950	1962	1950 to 1962
0 to 4	74.6	58.2	−22.0
5 to 7	85.0	74.6	−14.4
8	88.1	78.2	−12.7
9 to 11	92.1	88.8	−3.9
12	94.0	90.7	−3.7
13 to 15	79.6	83.0	+5.4
16 or more	92.1	92.3	+.2
All groups	87.6	83.5	−4.7

SOURCE: The 1950 labor force data are taken from appendix Table A1, and population data from the 1950 census. The 1962 figures are from unpublished data supplied by the U.S. Bureau of Labor Statistics.

This table tells us that the participation rates at the lower end of the educational scale, which were already relatively low in 1950, had gone much lower by 1962. At the other end of the scale, participation rates had gone up by 1962. (The reason why the increase for college graduates was so small is that even in 1950 their participation rates in the prime age groups—especially 25 to 54—were already quite high, in some categories 98 or 99 percent.) Some of the decline in participation rates at the lower end of the scale is due to higher average ages, with a larger proportion in this group (as compared with upper groups) attaining age 65 and voluntarily retiring. But that is by no means the whole story. A detailed comparison by age group as well as by educational level shows that declines occurred at almost every age level in the noncollege category, while there was a rise in participation rates for a majority of the age groups of men with college training.

The important point that I want to make with these figures is that in all likelihood the official unemployment statistics substantially understate the size of the labor surplus of men with limited education. If we found jobs for most of those now officially reported as unemployed, the news of improving opportunities would undoubtedly bring back into the labor force many men who are not now counted as members of it. Unfortunately, we cannot count on the same flexibility of supply at the top of the educational scale. Even the most extreme pressures of demand cannot pull the participation rate much above 98 or 99 percent, which (as just stated) is the current rate in some college-trained age groups.

Our overall unemployment rate has now been above 5 percent for more than 5 years, and we cannot be sure what effects a substantial increase in spending by consumers, businesses, and government (*i.e.*, an increase in aggregate demand) would have on the patterns of employment, unemployment, and labor force participation just discussed. Many respected economists believe, as one of them once put it, that the hard core of unemployment is made of ice, not rock, and that it would melt away if overall demand rose high enough. As already noted, the Council of Economic Advisers has virtually guaranteed that the administration's tax-cut program—which in its current version would put about $11 billion in the hands of consumers and businesses—would reduce unemployment to an "interim target" rate of 4 percent by 1966. This line of reasoning assumes (either implicitly or sometimes explicitly) that no serious bottlenecks of labor supply would appear before the achievement of the overall unemployment rate of 4 percent. I seriously question the validity of this critically important assumption under the labor market conditions of today and the foreseeable future.

The benefits of a decline in the overall rate of unemployment appear to be quite unevenly distributed among the educational attainment groups that we have been considering. The year 1957 was the last one in which we had an unemployment rate as low as 4 percent. It is instructive to see how the patterns of unemployment changed from 1950, when the overall rate was above 6 percent, to 1957, and then again to 1962, which had about the same overall rate as 1950. This comparison is made in two forms in table 3. This table shows the actual unemployment rates for the various educational attainment groups in those 3

TABLE 3. *Actual and Relative Unemployment by Educational Attainment, April 1950, March 1957, and March 1962 (males, 18 and over)*

Years of school completed	Unemployment rates					
	Actual percentages			Relative [a]		
	1950	1957	1962	1950	1957	1962
0 to 7	8.4	6.9	9.2	154	203	170
8	6.6	4.4	7.5	108	110	132
9 to 11	6.9	4.7	7.3	115	120	142
12	4.6	3.0	4.8	70	67	75
13 to 15	4.1	2.7	4.0	64	64	65
16 or more	2.2	.6	1.4	34	14	21
All groups	6.2	4.1	6.0	a	a	a

[a] The relative unemployment rate is the ratio between the percentage unemployment rate for a given educational attainment group and the percentage unemployment rate for all other groups at the same point in time.

SOURCES: Percentage unemployment figures from appendix Table A-3; relative unemployment rates computed from data in appendix Tables 19 and 20 [in original article].

years, and it also expresses the unemployment rate for each group in each of the 3 years as a ratio of the rate for all of the other groups combined. (Thus, the 0 to 7 years of education group had an unemployment rate about 50 percent higher than all other groups combined in 1950; its rate was more than double the rate for all other groups in 1957; and its rate was 70 percent higher in 1962.)

Clearly, unemployment at the bottom of the educational scale was relatively unresponsive to general increases in the demand for labor, while there was very strong responsiveness at the top of the educational scale. The percentage unemployment rate for college graduates in 1957 merits close attention. It was an almost incredible 0.6 percent. I have queried the experts in the Bureau of Labor Statistics on this figure, and they assure me that they have no less confidence in it than in the other 1957 figures. Surely a figure as low as that represents what is sometimes called "overfull" employment—*i.e.*, demand which seriously exceeds supply.

Bear in mind that the unemployment rates for the lower educational attainment groups (those with 80 percent of the men) are now higher than in 1950, and that the unemployment rate for college graduates is now substantially lower than in 1950. Also bear in mind that the labor force participation rate figures strongly suggest a large and growing "reserve army"—which is not counted among the unemployed—at the lower educational levels, and that there is no evidence of any such reserve of college-trained men. Finally, bear in mind the differences between the lower end of the educational scale and the upper end in responsiveness to overall decreases in the unemployment rate.

When you put all of these considerations together, I believe that you are ineluctably led to the conclusion that long before we could get down to an overall unemployment rate as low as 4 percent, we would have a severe shortage of workers at the top of the educational ladder. This shortage would be a bottleneck to further expansion of employment. I cannot pinpoint the level at which the bottleneck would begin to seriously impede expansion; but, on the basis of the relationships revealed by Table 3, it seems reasonable to believe that we could not get very far below a 5-percent over-all unemployment level without hitting that bottleneck.

The most fundamental conclusion that emerges from my analysis is that automation and the changing pattern of consumer wants have greatly increased the importance of investment in human beings as a factor in economic growth. More investment in plant and equipment, without very large increases in our investment in human beings, seems certain to enlarge the surplus of underdeveloped manpower and to create a shortage of the highly developed manpower needed to design, install, and man modern production facilities.

The Manpower Development and Training Act is aptly named, soundly conceived, and well administered. . . . But I doubt that even the most enthusiastic supporters of the Manpower Development and Training Act program (and I count myself among them) would argue that its present or projected size is really commensurate with the size of the job to be done. We ought to be thinking in terms of helping two or three times as many people as this program is now expected to reach. I do not imply any criticism of the Congress in this comment, because it is my strong impression that dollars are not the limiting factor in the development of the Manpower Development and Training Act program. The real shortage in most areas, I believe, is trained manpower—specifically, qualified instructors and program administrators. It would be pointless to double or triple the appropriations for the program if the extra money could not be spent, and I doubt that it could be. Here we have an example of a present shortage of highly trained manpower, a shortage that limits the possibility of investment to remedy the educational deficiencies of the past.

Let us consider another, somewhat similar example. As we have all heard over and over again, the outlook for high school dropouts is bleak indeed. Exhortations, no matter how well meant, are not going to cure this problem, and neither will the token fund set aside by President Kennedy for grants to local units for experimental programs in this area. But here again dollars alone are not the answer. We need many more highly skilled teachers, counselors, and social workers. These, too, are in very short supply. Many other present shortages of highly trained manpower, in the private sector of the economy as well as in the public, could be cited. Unquestionably, these shortages would be intensified and new ones would appear if we moved closer to full utilization of our economic potential.

To my mind, the greatest shortcoming of the administration's program for reducing unemployment is the failure to recognize the crucial need to break the trained manpower bottleneck. . . .

I would give a considerably higher priority to the stimulation of investment in human beings than I would to such measures as the proposed tax cut. But I would still rate the tax cut as important. Denying that the tax cut is the ultimate weapon against unemployment is not denying that it can make some contribution to the reduction of unemployment. After all, even to get below a 5-percent unemployment rate would be a considerable achievement today. But a really effective attack on the complex problem of unemployment requires a whole arsenal of powerful weapons.

And we don't have all the time in the world. Human history has been described as a race between education and catastrophe. In the past dozen years, education has been falling behind in that race.

Structural Unemployment

COUNCIL OF ECONOMIC ADVISERS

This is the Council's answer to the "structuralists" (including Charles Killingsworth). It was submitted to the Senate Subcommittee on Employment and Manpower of the Committee on Labor and Public Welfare, the same subcommittee that Killingsworth appeared before, and was then reprinted in the January 1964 Economic Report of the President.

RECENT DISCUSSIONS may have generated an impression of greater disagreement among the nation's economists about the origins and solutions of the employment problem than actually exists. For in fact, the great majority of those who have studied the matter carefully would agree with the Administration's view that our excessive unemployment today cannot be traced to a single cause nor eliminated by a single cure. Rather, it has a mixture of causes which must be dealt with by a mixture—an amalgam—of cures.

One problem, and a central one, is that total expenditures in the economy—total demand for goods and services—are not sufficient to generate an adequate total number of jobs. We can, for convenience, call this kind of unemployment "demand-shortage" unemployment. In our view, demand-shortage unemployment can and must be attacked by vigorous policies—principally tax reduction—to raise the total demand for goods and services.

Another problem is that the characteristics of our available workers—their locations, skills, education, training, race, sex, age, and so on—do not fully match the characteristics employers are seeking in filling the jobs that are available (or that would be available at full employment). In a dynamic, changing economy there is always some of this mismatching, and we call the unemployment that results from it "frictional." But when the pockets of such unemployment become large and stubborn—especially when they impose chronic burdens on particular disadvantaged groups and regions—we speak of the unemployment problem as "structural."

This type of unemployment is also a serious problem, which requires major policy actions to overcome its corrosive effects. Structural problems are not new. And the available evidence does not show that the proportion of our total unemployment problem that we label "structural" has increased significantly, nor that its character has materially changed. But this in no way diminishes the need for attacking these structural problems with vigorous policies—principally education, training and retraining, and special regional programs—to match the supply of labor skills more closely to the changing demand for labor skills.

Along with demand-shortage and structural unemployment, one also hears a great deal about the problem of "technological unemployment"—of men being put out of work by machines and, more particularly, by the process which has come to be called "automation." This is, indeed, a serious and continuing problem. But two points should be emphasized at the outset.

First, "technological unemployment" is not a third form of unemployment, separate from the other two. Rather, it expresses itself through these other forms. Technological change causes obsolescence of skills and therefore produces some of the mismatching between available workers and jobs that we call "structural" unemployment. Moreover, by raising output per worker, technological change is one of the principal sources of growth in our *potential* total output or GNP—which, if not matched by corresponding growth in *actual* GNP, opens a gap in demand and thereby causes demand-shortage unemployment.

Second, those who maintain that the economy now faces a problem of "technological unemployment" that is somehow new, and more formidable than in the past implicitly assert that the rate of technological change has recently speeded up. Unless this is the case, the problem is not new—it has always been with us and has not proved to be a long-run problem for the economy as a whole. The continuing process of rapid technological change, which has constituted the very core of the American economy's strength and progressiveness for at least 150 years, has always put particular workers and businesses out of jobs and required particular adjustments that have been difficult and sometimes painful. It poses a new general problem for the economy only if technological change becomes so rapid that the demand adjustments and labor market adjustments it requires cannot be accomplished by the economic processes of the past. Whether technological change indeed has accelerated, or is in process of accelerating, is a factual question.

These, then—demand-shortage elements, structural elements, and a possible aggravation of both by accelerated technological change—are the principal ingredients of the unemployment problem. It would be unwise and imprudent to ignore any of these ingredients either in diagnosing the problem or in prescribing remedies.

The primary attack on high unemployment must be through fiscal measures to speed the growth of total demand and thereby to create new job opportunities. But this need not—indeed, must not—impede a simultaneous attack on our stubborn structural problems. The two approaches are not merely complementary; they are mutually reinforcing. On the one hand, training and other programs to facilitate labor mobility can ease and speed the process by which demand-stimulated increases in output are translated into increases in employment. On the other, since structural maladjustments tend to flourish in slack markets, a vigorous expansion in demand helps cut structural problems down to size. . . .

THE PERSISTENT PROBLEMS OF STRUCTURAL UNEMPLOYMENT

A tax cut would increase demand to levels consistent with a 4-percent rate of unemployment. It would ease our most pressing unemployment problems. But no one can assume that our worries about unemployment would then be over. Some of its most distressing and inequitable aspects would remain.

To be sure, tax-reduction will create new jobs in every community across the nation and expand employment in every industry. The overwhelming majority of American families will benefit directly from the income tax cuts that will accrue to 50 million tax-paying individuals and 600,000 tax-paying corporations. Their direct rise in after-tax income will soon be translated, through the marketplace, into stronger markets for all kinds of goods and services and a quickening of the business pulse in all communities. With average working hours already at a high level, this added demand and activity will in large part be translated, in turn, into additional jobs, and income for the unemployed. Thus, the non-taxpaying minority will, in a very real sense, be the greatest beneficiaries of the tax program.

Experience clearly shows (1) that the unemployment rate will decline for every major category of workers and (2) that the sharpest declines will occur where the incidence of unemployment is the highest: among teenagers, the Negroes, the less-skilled, the blue-collar groups generally.

But even so, the unemployment rates of many groups will still be intolerably high. Back in 1957, for instance, when the average unemployment rate was just over 4 percent for the whole economy, the rates were much higher for many disadvantaged groups and regions—*e.g.*, 10.8 percent for teenagers, 8.0 percent for nonwhites, 9.4 percent for unskilled manual workers, and 11.5 percent for workers in Wilkes-Barre–Hazleton, Pennsylvania.

These *high specific unemployment rates, which persist even when the general rate falls to an acceptable level,* are the essence of the problem of structural unemployment. Even a fully successful tax cut cannot solve problems like these by itself. They require a more direct attack.

To reduce the abnormally high and stubborn unemployment rate for Negroes requires a major improvement in their education and training and an attack on racial discrimination. To reduce the persistent high rate for the unskilled and the uneducated groups demands measures to help them acquire skills and knowledge. To reduce excessive unemployment associated with declining industries and technological advance requires retraining and relocation. To reduce high unemployment in distressed areas of Pennsylvania, Michigan, Minnesota, and elsewhere calls for special measures to rebuild the economic base of those communities and assist their workers.

Both the Administration and the Congress have recognized that these measures must be taken concurrently with measures to expand aggregate demand. Coal miners in Harlan County are structurally unemployed *now,* and so are Negro and Puerto Rican youths in New York City. Yet, programs to reduce structural unemployment will run into severe limits *in the absence of an adequate growth of demand, i.e.,* in the absence of rapid expansion of total job opportunities. Such expansion is needed to assure that retrained and upgraded workers, for example, *will* find jobs at the end of the training period and *will not* do so at the expense of job opportunities for other unemployed workers. As structural programs create new and upgraded skills, they will in some cases fit the participants for jobs that had previously gone begging. But for the most part, the needed jobs must be created by expansion of total demand.

Quite apart from the human significance of structural unemployment, it also has great economic importance. For only as we reduce structural unemployment can we achieve the higher levels of total output which would be associated with unemployment rates below our 4-percent interim target.

Every worker needlessly unemployed represents a human cost which offends the sensibilities of a civilized society. But each worker needlessly unemployed also represents a waste of potential goods and services, which even an affluent society can ill afford. More intensive measures to attack structural unemployment are necessary to reduce the unemployment rate not merely to 4 percent, but beyond.

HAS STRUCTURAL UNEMPLOYMENT INCREASED?

The preceding section addressed itself to structural unemployment as a human and social problem and considered its role in the process of lowering the unemployment rate to and below 4 percent. But it is also appropriate to ask: has structural unemployment increased to such an extent since 1957—the last time unemployment was near 4 percent—that it will impede the expansionary effects of demand-creating measures in general and the tax cut in particular?

An affirmative answer would, we believe, represent a misreading of the facts. As we have already pointed out, there *are* serious structural problems, and prompt action is needed both to root out inequities and hardships they inflict and to help us reach our employment goals. But this conclusion need not—and does not—rest on a belief that there has been a disproportionate surge in structural unemployment since 1957.

A reading of the evidence on this score must focus principally on what happens, over time, to the unemployment rates of particular groups—teenagers, untrained and unskilled workers, Negroes, and other disadvantaged groups and regions—in relation to the total unemployment rate. It would clearly be misleading simply to compare unemployment rates for such groups in a year like 1957, when the total rate was about 4 percent, with the corresponding rates in 1962–63, when the total rate has averaged 5.6 percent. Rather, it is the *relationship* between the total rate and the groups' rates—and its historical development—that reveals whether the structural problem is getting worse or not. And this relationship has been remarkably stable.

The disadvantaged groups almost invariably share more than proportionately—and the skilled and white-collar groups less than proportionately—in both decreases and increases in total employment. In the past, when the over-all unemployment rate has risen (or fallen) 1 percentage point, the rate for nonwhites and teenagers has risen (or fallen) by about 2 percentage points, the rate for unskilled workers by about 2½ percentage points. But the rate for professional and technical workers has risen or fallen by only about one-fourth of a percentage point.

One obvious reason for the disproportionate impact on teenagers is that they are the most recent additions to the labor force. When new job opportunities are few, there is a backing-up at the point of entry. Furthermore, even when they do find jobs, they tend to have the lowest seniority and are therefore first to be laid off. Much the same is true of Negroes. Given existing patterns of discrimination, they are often in marginal jobs or at the bottom of seniority lists. Moreover, when jobs are scarce and labor is plentiful, racial discrimination, where it exists, is more likely to enter into hiring and firing decisions. And at such times, employers are also more inclined to pass over inexperienced and untrained workers and less inclined to press their own efforts to adapt such personnel to their needs via in-service training programs. They tend to be less aggressive in seeking new employees outside their own local labor markets. And labor supply considerations are less likely to determine the location of new plants.

On the other hand, employers do not typically discharge many supervisory and technical personnel when output drops and, as a result, they do not need to expand their employment of such persons proportionately when output rises.

Moreover, there are other reasons why the employment of many categories of workers does not rise and fall in the same proportion as the total. Some disparities arise from the com-

TABLE 1. *Change in Unemployment Rate, Selected Groups and Areas*

	1960-1961	1961-1962
Total	1.1%	−1.1%
Teenagers	1.6	−1.9
Nonwhites	2.3	−1.5
Nonfarm laborers	2.0	−2.1
Operatives	1.6	−2.1
Manufacturing workers	1.5	−1.9
Miners	2.1	−3.0
For illustrative purposes:		
Michigan	3.4	−3.4
Wheeling, W. Va.	6.9	−7.8

plex interrelationship between the composition and the level of total output. To cite just one example, the rate of inventory accumulation is highly sensitive to the rate of expansion or contraction in total output, and goods that typically are inventoried tend to require large numbers of production workers. In contrast, the service industries, whose output is not subject to inventory accumulation nor to such wide fluctuations in consumption, generally use more technical and white-collar workers.

Thus it is not surprising to find that slackened demand since 1957 has intensified inter-group and inter-regional disparities in unemployment rates at the same time that it raised the total unemployment rate. Nonwhites, teenagers, unskilled and semi-skilled workers have suffered a greater-than-average increase in unemployment since 1957. But these same groups will also benefit disproportionately as demand expands and the over-all unemployment rate declines. This point is illustrated in the table above, which shows how the incidence of unemployment changed during the 1960–1961 recession and the 1961–1962 recovery.

Studies of changes in the incidence of unemployment among unskilled and semi-skilled blue-collar workers—whose jobs would seem to be highly vulnerable to technological change—can provide important insights into the structural unemployment problem. One would expect an accelerated rate of technological displacement to be reflected in rising rates of unemployment for these groups—relative to total unemployment. One would also expect to find such a relative rise for workers in industries such as manufacturing, mining, and transportation where automation has so far found its widest application.

To test this possibility, we have correlated the unemployment rate in specific occupations and industries with the rate for all experienced workers in the labor force during the 1948–1957 period—in other words, for the period before the main structural unemployment upsurge is alleged to have occurred. These correlations were then used to calculate what the occupational and industrial distribution of unemployment *would* have been in 1962 if the old relationships had held. If there had been a substantial increase in structural maladjustments, the actual 1962 unemployment rates for what we may call the "technologically vulnerable groups" should have been *higher* than these calculated rates. But in fact, as Table 2 shows a majority of the rates are *lower*. For some of these occupations and industries,

TABLE 2. *Unemployment Rates in Industries and Occupations Most Vulnerable to Technical Displacement, 1957 and 1962*

Industry or occupation	1957	1962	Change in rate, 1957-62: Actual	Change in rate, 1957-62: Expected [a]
All workers	4.3%	5.6%	1.3%	–
Experienced wage and salary workers	4.5	5.5	1.0	–
Workers in selected industries (goods producing)	5.4	6.4	1.0	1.3%
Mining, forestry, and fisheries	6.3	8.6	2.3	1.8
Construction	9.8	12.0	2.2	1.8
Durable goods manufacturing	4.9	5.7	0.8	1.4
Nondurable goods manufacturing	5.3	5.9	0.6	1.0
Transportation and public utilities	3.1	3.9	0.8	1.0
Experienced workers	3.9	4.9	1.0	–
Workers in selected occupations (blue collar)	6.0	7.4	1.4	1.7
Craftsmen, foremen, and kindred workers (skilled)	3.8	5.1	1.3	1.3
Operatives and kindred workers (semi-skilled)	6.3	7.5	1.2	1.6
Laborers, except farm and mine (unskilled)	9.4	12.4	3.0	2.6

[a] Calculated by use of correlations of (1) unemployment rates by industry with the rate for all experienced wage and salary workers, and (2) unemployment rates by occupation with the rate for all experienced workers, using data for the period 1948-1957 in both cases.

SOURCES: Department of Labor and Council of Economic Advisers.

the actual increase in unemployment was greater than expected, but in most cases it was less. And taking all of the blue-collar occupations and goods-producing industries together, we also find that the rise in actual unemployment was somewhat less than the 1948–1957 experience would have suggested.

We do not conclude from this evidence, nor from similar findings by Edward Denison and Otto Eckstein [2] as to the *geographic* distribution of unemployment, that a reduction in structural unemployment has occurred. Similarly, however, we do not conclude that the unusually high unemployment rates experienced by teenagers this year, or the rather low rates experienced by adult males, prove an adverse structural shift. In some labor market areas, imbalances have lessened; in others they have increased. But this does not suggest that the over-all rate of structural unemployment has risen significantly.

One similar piece of evidence relates to job vacancies. Since structural unemployment is a form of joblessness that persists over a protracted period even if unfilled jobs are available, an increase in structural unemployment would be clearly suggested if it were found that the number of job vacancies were rising along with the number of unemployed men.

Unhappily we have no comprehensive and adequate series designed to measure job vacancies in the United States. The Department of Labor currently is proposing experimental work leading toward the eventual establishment of such a series. This is a proposal we strongly endorse, although we share the Labor Department's awareness that such a series involves many technical problems and will need to be interpreted with care, especially in its early years.

But meanwhile the only available indicator that bears upon the job-vacancy situation is the National Industrial Conference Board's index of the number of help-wanted advertisements published in the classified section of a leading newspaper in each of 33 leading labor market areas. While this series does a good

2. Edward F. Denison, *The Incidence of Unemployment by States and Regions, 1950 and 1960*, and *The Dispersion of Unemployment Among Standard Metropolitan Statistical Areas, 1950 and 1960*. Mimeograph. Otto Eckstein, *The Unemployment Problem in Our Day*, paper delivered before the Conference on Unemployment and the American Economy, Berkeley, California, April 1963.

job of reporting what it is designed to report, obviously it provides a comparatively sketchy and imperfect indication of job vacancies. All the same, it is interesting that, after adjustment for changes in the size of the labor force, the help-wanted index was substantially lower in 1960 and 1962 than in 1955–1957, when the total unemployment rate was about 4 percent. We have further adjusted the index for changes in the total unemployment rate in order to screen out the effects of slack demand. Even in this form the index fails to rise significantly since 1957—as one would expect it to do if underlying structural unemployment had broadened.

The evidence reviewed above does not yield persuasive indications that structural elements are today a significantly larger factor in our unemployment than in 1957. Nevertheless, it would not be surprising if some particular aspects of structural unemployment have intensified. One would assume that the longer a period of slack persists, the more likely it would be that the detailed structure of skills, experience, and training of the labor force would fail to reflect fully the pattern of job requirements at high levels of employment. High employment in 1967 will call for a somewhat different pattern of jobs than existed in 1957, and a slack labor market does not accurately foretell what that pattern will be. Moreover, there is danger that, after a long period of slack, new hiring standards, habits of mind, and expectations appropriate to an "easy" labor market will have become entrenched, rationalizing increased discriminations against disadvantaged groups. Thus, after the period of prolonged slack since 1957, there is more need than in the usual "cyclical" recovery for an effective program of specific labor-market policies to assist demand-stimulating policies in tailoring men to jobs and jobs to men.

SHIFTING EDUCATIONAL REQUIREMENTS AND BOTTLENECKS

In recent weeks—partly before this Committee, partly elsewhere—particular attention has been given to one aspect of the problem of structural maladjustments. This is the question of whether a recent shift in the pace and character of technological change has accelerated the long-term rise in job educational and skill requirements in a way that imposes a new bottleneck on expansion. The issue merits special discussion because of the obstacle to the employment-expanding effects of the tax program that this skilled-manpower bottleneck is alleged to present.

The argument is that the nature of recent technological change has caused a rapid shift in the pattern of manpower demand, pushing down the demand for workers with little training and pushing up the demand for the highly educated. Everyone agrees that the educational level of the nation's population has continued to advance, causing the supply of highly educated manpower to grow rapidly, and the supply of relatively uneducated manpower to decline. Thus the concern expressed is not about keeping pace with an absolute increase in job educational requirements—which have been rising right along—but about being unable to keep pace with an abrupt recent rise in such requirements.

It is feared that as demand increases, there will not be enough highly educated workers to fill the key technical and professional positions that must be manned if production is to expand to levels consistent with 4 percent unemployment; that, in consequence, expansion of output will be frustrated; and that, because of this, high percentages of the remainder of the labor force—including poorly educated workers—will be left unemployed.

It is important to distinguish this quite specific point about near-term bottlenecks from other propositions about the economic importance of education. It is unquestionably true, we believe, that greatly reinforced education is needed to press the attack on the pockets of long-term structural unemployment that have plagued the economy for a long time.

It is unquestionably true, moreover, that educational attainment enormously affects the employment prospects of the individual. Whether the economy is booming or stagnating, the poorly educated always come off second best. A grade school graduate is 5 times likelier to be unemployed than is a college graduate. Today's school dropouts are tomorrow's unemployed.

It is further well-known that long-term shifts, which can be projected to continue, in the relative importance of various industries, and long-term trends in technological development, are, on the whole, raising (as well as altering) educational requirements. *The Report on Manpower Requirements, Re-*

sources, Utilization, and Training by Secretary of Labor Willard Wirtz last March indicated the nature of these continuing shifts, including projections by broad groups to 1970 and 1975. The clearly indicated rise in the requirement for professional, technical, and kindred workers—teachers, scientists, physicians, engineers, technicians, and nurses—pose obvious demands on education in general and higher education in particular. And increased demands for many special skills create needs for expanded programs of vocational education and for more persons with a basic high school education. These long-term trends are not at issue in the present discussion.

The statistical testing of the educational bottleneck hypothesis turns out, if properly done, to be a very complex undertaking. There are problems of the noncomparability between decennial census data and information drawn from current population surveys; of the lack of appropriate annual series; of calculating appropriate current full-employment labor-force participation rates for particular age and educational-attainment groups instead of arbitrarily projecting the rates of a remote year; and of including not merely the male but the female components of our population. . . .

However, some reliable impressions already have emerged from the figures at hand. One is that, while there does appear to have been some rise in the demand for highly educated workers relative to their supply during the postwar period *as a whole*, the timing of this change is crucial for purposes of evaluating the bottleneck thesis. Since the economy operated at approximately a 4 percent unemployment rate in the mid-50s without encountering serious skilled-manpower bottlenecks the key question is whether most of this shift occurred *before* or after the 1955–1957 period. Hence a shift in job educational requirements relative to supply that had occurred before those years, and was not serious enough to obstruct expansion then, poses little threat to a new move back toward 4 percent unemployment now.

The available unemployment data seems to show that whatever shift may have occurred in job educational requirements relative to supply *did* occur prior to 1957. Indeed it may have been partially reversed since that time. From 1957 to 1962, for example, the unemployment rate for male workers with an 8th grade education or less rose by about one-half, roughly the same as the rate of overall unemployment. But the unemployment rate for college graduates rose from 0.6 percent to 1.4 percent.

In addition to unemployment rates, the percentages of labor-force participation by groups of different educational attainments also have changed during the postwar period. Here the data currently in hand do not permit us to locate the timing of these changes to the degree that has been possible with the unemployment rates. And so we simply do not know whether here, too, the shift toward greater participation by the well-educated, and lesser participation by the poorly educated, may largely have occurred before 1957.[3]

If, in the absence of information, one assumes that the shift in relative participation rates occurred more recently, one might conclude that there have been some withdrawals from the labor force by poorly educated male workers. Whenever they occurred, they present an obvious challenge to both public and private training programs. But the magnitude of these shifts is easily exaggerated—especially if one fails to make adequate allowance for the improvements in retirement programs during the past dozen years. It is clear that the vast majority of the so-called "losses" of less educated workers from the male labor force were concentrated in the 65-and-older age group.

In any event, none of this goes to the real nub of the issue. That nub is the failure of the bottleneck hypothesis to make any allowance for the proven capacity of a free labor market—especially one endowed with a high average level of education and enterprise and expanding programs to improve labor skills and mobility—to reconcile discrepancies between particular labor supplies and particular labor demands.

If relative shortages of particular skills develop, the price system and the market will moderate them, as they always have done in the past. Employers will be prompted to step up their in-service training programs and, as more jobs become available, poorly skilled and poorly educated workers will be more strongly motivated to avail themselves of training, retraining, and adult education opportunities. Government manpower programs begun

3. From data examined since the testimony was prepared, it appears that the shift toward greater participation by the well educated primarily occurred before 1957; as to the poorly educated, roughly half of the shift toward lower participation occurred prior to and half after 1957.

in the 1961–1963 period will also be operating to help ease the adjustment of specific shortages.

As for the personnel with the very highest skills, many—for the very reason that they are scarce—have been "stockpiled" by their employers and are not working to capacity when business is slack. As business picks up, they will be used more fully—and they will be used more efficiently. As engineers become scarce, and more expensive, their talents will be concentrated on engineering assignments, leaving drafting (for example) for draftsmen, who can be trained more quickly.

Naturally, most college graduates will have jobs no matter how high the unemployment rate in the whole economy, even if they have to work below the level for which they are qualified. If they are already in the supervisory or technical jobs for which they are best qualified, their employers will not have to increase by 10 percent the number of such jobs in order to increase total employment by 10 percent. And to the extent that they are not already in such jobs, they are a hidden reservoir of superior talent.

The highly-educated-manpower-bottleneck argument arrives at its alarming conclusion by projecting to new situations a perfectly static set of educational requirements. The argument makes no allowance for flexibility in the system. Flexibility, of course, is not unlimited. If we were talking about accomplishing a massive increase in output within a few months, manpower bottlenecks might indeed become critical. But we find it unrealistic to believe that they represent a major constraint upon an extra $30 billion of output in what will soon be a $600 billion economy—especially when (*a*) there are virtually no current signs of tension in either labor markets or product markets and (*b*) the demand expansion that will accomplish the closure will be spread over 2 or more years in which continuing new supplies of highly trained manpower will be entering the labor market.

Earlier the question was raised whether structural elements in unemployment have grown so much since 1957 that they threaten to impede an economic expansion induced by the tax cut. We have examined this question from a number of directions, and we now summarize our answer.

The answer is clear: The evidence we have assembled and the

tests we have made do not support the thesis that, over-all, the incidence of structural unemployment has increased in importance since we last achieved high employment. There may be some problems that seem more serious today than earlier; but in other areas we have probably progressed.

Expansion of the economy in response to a stepping-up of the growth of demand will not be impeded by pockets of surplus labor existing in a limited number of categories—we have always had distressing surpluses in certain categories, and the tax cut will not fully eliminate them. Economic expansion could eventually be impeded by shortages in strategic categories of skills and training, but the statistical evidence reveals no such shortages enroute to 4 percent unemployment.

It is difficult to believe that an economy that was able to absorb the dramatic shifts needed to convert to war production in World War II, and that operated at unemployment levels as low as 1.2 percent during that war and more recently (1953) at 2.9 percent, could not move rather readily, over the space of 2 or 3 years, to our interim target of 4 percent unemployment.

Unsatisfied as we all must be with our nation's achievements in education—and with the distressing problem of school dropouts—we must not disregard the fact that our labor force today is better educated and, as a result, more flexible than ever before. The median level of education among the adult male members of the labor force has risen by an astonishing 50 percent since the beginning of World War II. New entrants into the labor force are on the average better equipped than ever before to respond to a changing pattern of demand. By 1966, when the full effects of the tax cut will be apparent, the ranks of trained workers will have been swelled by two more annual graduating classes from our high schools, colleges, and professional and graduate schools. In each case, the size of the groups will dwarf all previous records.

Our own recent economic history assures us of the economy's ability to adapt to rapid change. Additional assurance along this line is found in the experience of other countries whose systems and values are similar to our own. During the past decade, the Western European economy has undergone staggering structural changes. France and Belgium have adjusted to the decline of important mining areas, Germany to the inflow of millions of refugees from the East, and Italy to the problem of absorbing large numbers of poorly educated rural migrants into urban occupations. And all of Western Europe has adjusted to the replacement of obsolete capital, and of productive methods often unchanged for a century or more with machinery and methods geared to the most advanced technology in the world. The advance of productivity has been revolutionary. During the 1950s, output per manufacturing worker increased 2¼ times as fast in Germany as in the United States, 3 times as fast in France, and 4 times as fast in Italy. In their adjustment to these changes the Europeans, though they may have other advantages, did not have the advantage of a labor force nearly as well educated, as well trained, as mobile, or as flexible as ours.

Nonetheless, the Europeans have maintained unemployment rates considerably lower than ours. After adjustment for conceptual differences, the unemployment rate in 1960 was 1.0 percent in Germany, 1.9 percent in France, and 4.3 percent in Italy. In Italy and Germany these low rates represented a considerable improvement over earlier postwar experience, and the higher Italian rate has subsequently declined materially.

The major explanation for such low unemployment rates in economies undergoing such profound transitions lies in the maintenance of a very high level of demand. During the 1950s the average annual growth rate in France was 4 percent, in Italy, 6 percent, and in Germany, over 7 percent—and both Italy and France have had even higher rates so far in the 1960s. This experience demonstrates beyond any doubt that, under the stimulus of adequate demand, and with the aid of active labor market policies, modern economies are sufficiently resilient to absorb poorly educated workers, to adapt to skill shortages, and to adjust to rapid technological change in a manner which maintains extremely low unemployment rates. This European experience—which in broad outline has been matched in Japan—reassures us that, once high and growing demand presses our capacity, we too will adapt to rapid change and maintain our economic health.

Structural unemployment is a human and an economic problem that we must attack by every means available. But the expansion of total demand through tax reduction remains the crucial central element in our attack upon unemployment.

Shorter Hours: Tool to Combat Unemployment

AMERICAN FEDERATION OF LABOR AND CONGRESS OF INDUSTRIAL ORGANIZATIONS

The viewpoint of the AFL-CIO on shorter hours is well expressed in this statement, which is an abridged version of a pamphlet issued in 1963. The introduction is by George Meany.

IT IS APPARENT from the government figures issued in January [1963], that we are heading into our sixth straight year of substantial unemployment—that is, with 5 per cent or more of the labor force out of work. And, unfortunately, the most reasonable prediction is that matters will get worse in the months ahead.

In August 1962, the AFL-CIO Executive Council unanimously decided to press for a reduction in the basic workweek to 35 hours. It is hardly a satisfaction to note that, if anything, this is more valid now than it was then. For the nation's sake, and our own, we would rather have been wrong.

In summary, the case presented here is this:

First, there is nothing sacred about the 40-hour week; a periodic cut in working hours has been part of the American experience for the last century and has been proceeding even since the 40-hour standard was set.

Second, no one—certainly not the AFL-CIO—maintains that under ordinary circumstances 40 hours a week are excessive on grounds of health, safety or undue restriction of leisure time. On the contrary, the labor movement would be delighted if 40 hours of work were available to all who wanted them.

Third, it seems clear beyond question that 40-hour jobs will not be available to all Americans under presently foreseeable circumstances. This means a continuation of the intolerably high unemployment we have suffered for five full years.

Fourth, a cut in hours to 35 a week, while troublesome in some industries and occupations, could generally be handled without great difficulty and without a profoundly inflationary effect.

These four points, which this [article] documents, lead us to believe that a 35-hour week, with increased penalty pay to discourage overtime, is essential to the present and future economic health of the United States and therefore of the free world.

Our campaign is unique in that it is based wholly upon the intellectual grounds of the public welfare. It includes no horror stories of exploited, exhausted wage-earners dropping beside their machines. These may still be with us but the 40-hour week is not to blame.

We argue only that the prosperity of the United States must be based upon full employment and we believe full employment is possible only if the standard workweek is cut.

The recognition and acceptance of this argument will be proof of America's maturity in meeting its own problems and those it must shoulder in the world of today. GEORGE MEANY

TRENDS IN EMPLOYMENT AND UNEMPLOYMENT

American workers have always sought full employment at good wages. Since 1953, however, an increasing number have been denied the opportunity of achieving this objective.

Production and sales have risen at a slow pace. The spread of automation has made it possible to increase output with less manpower. At the same time the labor force has been expanding. The inevitable result has been rising unemployment and part-time work—a short workweek for many people and a workweek of zero hours for many more.

Unfortunately, improvements in this situation have not been forthcoming. One recession has followed fast upon another in these past nine years and the upturns between slumps have been getting weaker.

Workers have borne the brunt of these economic failures through a continuing and tragic trend of recurring layoffs, part-time work schedules and an insufficient number of new job opportunities for a growing labor force. The number of unemployed has risen from 1.9 million or 2.9 percent of the labor force in 1953, to 4 million or 5.6 percent of the labor force in 1962. The number of people on part-time work schedules because fulltime jobs are not available has continued to increase. In each month but one since November 1957, unemployment has been 5 percent or more of the labor force. . . .

The outlook for employment and unemployment in the period ahead remains bleak. On the basis of the government's estimate of sales and production in 1963, unemployment will increase from 5.6 percent of the labor force to 6 percent or more. Government officials have stated that, even if [the administration's] programs are adopted, they do not expect unemployment to decline to a 4-percent level—about 3 million jobless—before the middle of 1965 or 1966. Even these predictions may prove to be optimistic, particularly if Congress frustrates the Kennedy Administration's job-creating programs.

Present trends, therefore, spell continuing danger for the national economy. The government's programs to boost sales and production are, at best, inadequate to create jobs fast enough. At the same time, automation is spreading—even in offices, warehousing and retail trade, where employment increased substantially between 1953 and 1962. And the growth of the labor force is stepping up.

Expansionary government policies are needed—federal tax, expenditure and monetary policies—to boost sales, production and employment rapidly and to achieve full employment as soon as possible. The government's programs, thus far, have been inadequate. The goal of full employment has been pushed into the future.

Reduced working hours may not be the best way to create jobs. But shorter working hours can and will spread employment, to some extent. And neither government officials, business leaders nor university economists have presented any other practical alternatives for the increasing number of working people who are unemployed or who face layoffs.

Confronted with this situation, a faster pace of reducing working hours than in the past 20 years is essential—not as a panacea or ideal solution for unemployment, but simply as one step towards increasing the number of job opportunities.

THE LONG TREND TO SHORTER HOURS

A shorter workweek would take America the way of Rome; it would promote idleness instead of industriousness; it is impractical; it would undermine the social structure; it would make America "more vulnerable to the economic onslaughts of Europe."

These were the arguments of the 1920s against the five-day, 40-hour week. Today's arguments against shorter working hours may sound more rational, but the historical record shows they will in time probably appear as ludicrous as the moralistic and fearful arguments of the past.

Union proposals for shorter hours of work are hardly new. "Shorter hours" has been a recurrent bargaining and legislative issue since the Revolutionary War. But the demands of old for a 10-hour workday, and then 8 hours and the 5-day week, have become the demands of today for the 35-hour week.

Examination of hours reduction since the turn of the century reveals the following facts which may offer helpful perspectives for today's discussion of work hours:

1. The reduction in the workweek since the late 1930s has lagged far behind the trend in earlier decades of this century. In nearly four decades from 1900 to the mid-1930s, the generally prevailing fulltime workweek was shortened by 20 hours (from 60 to 40) or at a rate of roughly 5 hours a decade. Since the National Recovery Act (NRA) program in 1933–1935 set 40 hours as the new workweek standard, however, nearly 30 years have passed with no further general reduction in the workweek.

2. Although 40 hours have remained the typical workweek, shorter fulltime weeks already are in effect to a much greater extent than is generally recognized.

A reasonable estimate is that 10 to 15 percent of American nonagricultural wage and salary workers—between 5.5 and 8 million workers—are now on fulltime workweeks shorter than 40 hours, mostly 37.5 or 35 hours.

3. Both collective bargaining and governmental action have served as vehicles for hours reduction in the past. Collective bargaining's role is generally recognized, but government action also has played a key part by (*a*) developing reduction in specific areas (railroads and government work, for example) and for women and minors; (*b*) encouraging reductions during World War I and the Great Depression; and (*c*) formalizing and spreading the 40-hour standard in the late 1930s after it already had been widely adopted.

There have been notable specific examples of unilateral voluntary reductions by employers, but employer-initiated action has not produced general hours reduction in this century.

4. Employers traditionally and consistently have opposed

shorter hours. Their attitudes have not been a guide either to the economic or social desirability or to the practicability of hours reduction. The unqualified opposition typical in the last century and early part of this one has shifted in more recent years, however, to more sophisticated arguments that reduction may be sound—but only at some unspecified future period.

5. Reduction in the nation's prevailing hours schedules has come for the most part in spurts and in large amounts rather than gradually. About three-quarters of the 20 hours by which the standard workweek has been reduced since 1900 are accounted for by sizable cuts in rather short periods of time, during World War I and the early 1930s.

6. The timing and amount of reduction have not been economy-wide, however. Broad industry variations have persisted. Even in the two periods of most widespread change, the general reduction did not extend to some industries.

7. The form of reduction also has varied. Early in the century, the principal reduction was in hours per day, in moves from 10 to 9 to 8. Then came cuts in the number of days per week as Saturday was cut to a half day to make a 5.5-day workweek or eliminated altogether for a 5-day workweek. More recent attention has been directed mainly to new cuts in hours per day, particularly to a 7-hour standard.

The 1940s and 1950s have brought some hours reduction, not in the workweek, but in a new form—paid vacations and holidays, to provide a different type of increased leisure. Averaged over the year, present levels of paid vacations and holidays are somewhat less than 2.5 hours a week.

8. The reasons for hours reduction have shifted over the years. Efforts to shorten the 10-hour day were explained largely by social factors. Shorter hours were sought to permit leisure for family and social needs and to curtail the physical strain and hazards of excessive hours. Economic considerations, although often cited, were usually secondary.

The move to the 5-day week, however, was sought primarily for economic reasons, to help maintain and stimulate employment. Current proposals for workweeks shorter than 40 hours are similarly rooted mainly in the desire for increased employment security. . . .

REDUCING HOURS: CHOICES AND COSTS

To cut the workweek with no loss in weekly pay requires an increase in hourly pay. How much of an increase? If the hours cut is sizable, the increase will be rather substantial.

If the workweek were to be cut from 40 hours to 35 hours, the increase in hourly wages needed to provide the same pay received for 40 hours would be 14.3 percent.

For a specific example in dollar-and-cents terms, if hourly wages average $2.50, so weekly pay for 40 hours is $100, a reduction in hours to 35 would require an hourly increase of almost 36 cents to maintain weekly wages at $100. If the hours reduction in this example were only to 37½ hours, the hourly increase needed to maintain weekly pay would be 17 cents.

The percent of hourly increase required to maintain pay upon various reductions from 40 hours is shown below:

Cut from 40 hours to:	Increase in hourly pay to maintain same weekly pay
39	2.6%
38	5.3
37½	6.7
36	11.1
35	14.3
32	25.0

Can such hourly wage increases—say the sizable 14.3 percent involved in reduction from 40 to 35 hours—be taken in stride by industry? The answer depends on many factors and will vary industry by industry.

Major cost factors affecting ability to pay include:

1. The rate of productivity advance. The greater the rate of productivity advance, the more readily higher wage costs would be offset by increases in output per hour. Increasing momentum in technological and scientific advances serving to displace labor are enabling increased rates of productivity gain—and also making for reduced labor costs.

2. The industry's cost structure. The significance of labor costs in relation to material, capital and other costs is important. Where labor costs are a small part of total costs, a substantial

increase in wages may be readily absorbable. On the other hand, where labor content of the cost structure is high, there will be greater difficulty.

3. The type and extent of changes induced in equipment, methods and products. A marked change in hours probably would generate special re-examination and revision of various practices with consequent cost savings.

4. Demand levels and trends. Increased demand leads to expanded production and sales volume and thereby spreads overhead expenses over more units. Such reduction in unit costs are a major factor in offsetting increased labor costs.

5. Rate of use of plant and equipment. This is related to demand levels. If plant and equipment can be put to more intensive use—installation of an additional shift is a major example—savings in capital and overhead costs per unit ordinarily would be substantial and would counteract upward change in labor costs.

6. Effects on various labor costs. Reductions in hours may, by reducing need for layoffs and by improving attendance, safety and health, create savings in costs of unemployment compensation and layoff benefits, workmen's compensation and health and welfare benefits.

In addition to these basic cost factors, there are other considerations influencing financial ability to reduce hours with no loss in pay.

1. *Profits.* To the extent that costs are not fully offset by savings, they may be taken in stride by drawing on profits, particularly in highly profitable industries.

2. *Prices.* To the extent not met by savings or redistribution of profits, higher costs may be offset through price increases. Whether any price increases would be necessary depends on how all these listed factors work out.

3. *Gradualness of hours reduction.* A major element in absorbability would be whether the reduction was put into effect fully at one time or spread gradually in steps over a period of some months or years.

4. *Government programs.* Adjustment to increased costs required by shorter hours could be eased if new programs were developed to spread costs of reduction through use of a special tax and fund in the manner applied to meet costs of unemploy-

ment compensation and social security old-age benefits or to provide various types of preferred treatment—incentives—to firms shortening hours.

Industries which have a high rate of technological innovation, have high capital investment per worker and have expanding markets, should readily be able to handle substantial hours reductions. Industries with a high labor cost content and with declining markets may have a greater problem in maintaining weekly pay for substantially reduced workweeks.

The general state of the economy is obviously of crucial importance in many of these cost variables. Economic measures effectively stimulating a high growth rate would materially smooth the path for shorter hours—and would, by improving the unemployment picture, confine the need for hours reductions.

High levels of unemployment are not costless. Although not feasible to a break down on a company or industry basis in a cost accounting manner, the economic and social costs of unemployment to the community (including business) are considerable. To the extent that shorter hours ward off layoffs and aid in reemployment, it reduces these society-wide expenses and thereby helps finance its own costs.

Available studies on the relation of number of work-hours to productivity deal largely with workweeks longer than 40 hours. In general, they have found that fewer hours makes a man more productive each hour.

Past studies of the interrelation of hours and productivity emphasize the variations by type of work and type of workers. On machine-paced jobs, shorter hours may permit a somewhat faster pace since the pace need not be maintained over as long a period. Where the work pace is within control of the worker, there can be wide variation, often with marked increases in productivity. Much depends on the strenuousness, degree of concentration and attentiveness, and the monotony involved. The age and interest and, to some extent, perhaps, the sex of the particular worker and the climate of labor-management relations also will determine the extent to which fewer hours of work will increase performance each hour.

During the depression 1930s a number of instances of reduction to 6-hour-day, 36-hour weeks were reported on in detail. At the Kellogg Company of Battle Creek, Michigan, introduction of a 6-hour day in 1930 reportedly reduced fatigue, curtailed the accumulation of monotony which limited output during a longer day and reduced some "waste of time." A summary of experience with the 6-hour day at the India Tire and Rubber Company cited similar improvements and made special note of savings from a cutback in absenteeism.

Shorter hours will in the long run contribute to further gains in productivity. Much depends on how increased time off-work is put to use. But judging from the past, if increased leisure is widely used to stimulate educational development and to broaden the interests and outlook of workers and their children, the nation's productive powers will be greatly enhanced.

Though not measurable in dollar-and-cents terms, good use of increased leisure is a form of capital investment yielding future productivity returns. As one sociologist expressed it, "the improvement of human resources and their utilization through hygiene, education, recreation, and the heightened exercise of imagination make a contribution to economic growth which is commonly underestimated if not ignored."

The shorter hours issue is often described as a choice between income or leisure: "We can have either more income or more leisure, but not both."

If the nation wants more goods (and workers want more income), then hours should not be cut, this view states. It usually goes on to add that the nation needs more production to meet its domestic needs and world responsibilities and most workers prefer more income, as shown by the desire of many for overtime work and the taking of second jobs (so-called moonlighting). The conclusion of this reasoning is that shorter hours would be unwise and would reflect the desires of only a minority.

Many individuals, it is true, see the question of hours in this way. But the reason shorter hours arises now as a national issue is not because of a national re-examination of leisure but because of concern about the need for combatting actual and threatened unemployment. To cast the issue merely as income versus leisure is to skirt the overriding issue—unemployment.

The nation has been reducing hours, not by reducing the 40-hour week but by adding to unemployment (a no-hour workweek for these workers) and to involuntary part-time employment. The growth in unemployment is a form of increased "leisure" harmful to those affected and to the economy as a whole.

The issue is not leisure, but whether general shortening of the length of the standard workweek would be a useful tool in preventing and overcoming the no-hour workweeks of the many unemployed.

The need for additional production depends not merely on the length of the workweek but on the number employed. If the nation had full employment, then hours reduction would cut national output. But with high unemployment, a cut in hours would result in more work performed by those now not working. Holding fast to existing hours schedules while millions of workers are idle or only partly employed is obviously not the road to increased national production.

It is true that if workers are asked merely to choose between more income or more leisure most would select more income. But it is equally true that if asked to choose between more income or increased job security, between cutting men or cutting hours, the great majority of workers woud prefer increased job security.

Worker preference for security-increasing measures over additional income has been demonstrated repeatedly and increasingly in the growing bargaining emphasis on measures to avoid layoffs, to provide income for the unemployed and to develop health and welfare benefit programs.

Is additional overtime pay the real objective sought by some unions demanding shorter hours? Are shorter-hours demands merely a subterfuge for securing more income through increased overtime-pay hours? This is a criticism leveled by some opponents of hours reduction.

Any union and industry in a position to reduce hours, maintain weekly pay and then, instead of hiring more workers, work the former schedule with overtime pay for hours beyond the new standard are in an enviable economic position. If their objective is simply more pay rather than shorter hours and more employment, wages can be readily increased without a roundabout tinkering with the standard workweek.

Hours of Work

CLYDE E. DANKERT

Clyde E. Dankert is professor of economics at Dartmouth College. He has written extensively on hours of work, and the present selection is taken from his statement before a Congressional committee in June 1963.

OVER THE YEARS a great many arguments have been used in support of shorter hours. The particular argument that is given prominence at any particular time is closely related to the conditions, particularly the economic conditions, prevailing at the time, and so we have had the citizenship argument, the health argument, the greater production argument, the unemployment argument, the welfare argument, and so on.

At the present time, as we are all well aware, it is the unemployment argument that is in the forefront, and quite correctly so. This particular argument has been discussed on frequent occasions in times past. I like to recall the statement that Samuel Gompers, first president of the American Federation of Labor made back in 1887. This statement is somewhat of a classic and is sometimes quoted in observations relating to hours and mechanization. In his annual report to the AFL Mr. Gompers declared in 1887: "The displacement of labor by machinery in the past few years has exceeded that of any like period in our history."

Then, after citing various examples of mechanization of that time, Gompers went on to say: "The answer to all opponents to the reduction of the hours of labor could well be given in these words: That so long as there is one man who seeks employment and cannot obtain it, the hours of labor are too long."

It is very interesting to note that 2 years later Mr. Gompers made another statement to the AFL on the same theme. Here he referred to "the hundreds of thousands of our fellows, who through the ever-increasing inventions and improvements are rendered 'superfluous.'" Then he went on to say: "We must find employment for our wretched brothers and sisters by reducing the hours of labor or we will be overwhelmed and destroyed."

The unemployment argument for shorter hours is certainly not without some merit, particularly if hours of work are temporarily reduced. But it is my feeling that any sizable and particularly any permanent cut in hours just now would be economically unwise, largely ineffective in meeting the problem of structural unemployment, and, in the light of our present international situation, politically inexpedient. . . .

1. First of all, I think we should be aware of the simple fact that over the past years the length of the workweek for many workers, particularly in manufacturing, has been reduced from somewhere around 70 hours to about 40, and yet despite this remarkable decrease in the length of the work period, there doesn't seem to have been any reduction in the amount of unemployment in the country. Of course, it is true that a decrease in the length of the workday, or workweek, will reduce the volume of unemployment temporarily, but in terms of the permanent long-run effect there doesn't seem to have been much effect.

Thus, if there was a close connection between the length of the work period and the volume of unemployment we, with some justice, could expect to see that effect apparent in our unemployment figures.

To be sure, of course there were other influences operative during this period, but, nevertheless, if there was an important connection between hours and unemployment the permanent effects should be visible, at least to some extent.

But this lack of connection between the volume of unemployment and the length of the work period is not, in my estimation, surprising since the root causes of unemployment seem to have no particular relationship to the length of the work period.

For example, cutting hours does not do away with the factors bringing about cyclical fluctuations in business activity, with the causes of seasonality in industry, with the elements that lead to technological and other kinds of structural changes in our economy. All these influences in our society can operate just as effectively and just as disastrously with short hours as with long hours.

In other words, and to state the matter in a rather extreme form, but a form that is nevertheless true, we can have as much unemployment with a 30-hour week or a 35-hour week as with a 40-hour week or a 50-hour week.

I would like to say that when we move from one hour level or plateau to another, the amount of unemployment may well decrease. I think it probably would. And certainly this is all to the good. It is "a consummation devoutly to be wished." However, and this is the point I would like to emphasize, when we become adjusted to the new hour standards the causes of unemployment are as operative as they were before. That is, of course, unless we take other steps to cope with these causes.

2. Secondly, a general cut in the standard workweek to 35 hours would not provide, even temporarily, the number of new jobs that one might expect. One of our most outstanding labor leaders some time ago spoke of 5 million new jobs being created with a reduction in hours to 35. This result, presumably, would come from the transference of 175 million man-hours a week from 35 million present workers to the 5 million new workers.

I believe this general argument assumes a degree of occupational and geographical labor mobility that does not exist. For one thing, in many industries there would be technical difficulties in the way because of the highly fixed relationships that exist in many types of work between men and machines. For example, one man and one man only is needed to operate a bandsaw in a furniture factory. What would be done with the extra manpower brought into the plant? It may be that a second shift might be introduced, but this would give rise to various difficulties. . . . I believe the argument assumes an unduly high degree of similarity in skills and ability.

What is more, the policy would run into difficulties because of variations in the percentages of unemployment from industry to industry. A worker cannot easily shift from the shoe industry to the electronics industry.

Another difficulty is the variation that exists in the unemployment from area to area. Here, as a student of Adam Smith, I must use the occasion to quote a famous statement that Adam Smith made back in 1776 which is pertinent to this last point; namely, that "man is of all forms of luggage the most difficult to be transported." This is true today despite the progress we have made in the way of transportation facilities, including railways, steamships, and planes.

Then there is another reason why the number of workers finding employment, as a consequence of reducing hours to 35 a week, would not be as large as one might expect. This is the practice of moonlighting. I would not like to exaggerate the extent to which this would be encouraged by a cut in hours. However, it seems to me that some workers would take up a second or third job, and, of course, this would be to the disadvantage of those who are still unemployed.

Finally, instead of taking on new workers, employers may work their present employees longer hours, even at the cost of rather heavy overtime pay. Because of the costs involved in hiring and employing new workers, including the payment of various fringe benefits, employers may find it economically expedient to go onto an overtime basis and, as a matter of fact, a considerable number of employers have already done this and we hear reports of some workers working 60 or more hours a week while others are unemployed.

I believe that if the standard workweek were reduced to 35 hours with time-and-a-half beginning at 35 hours, the extent of moonlighting might well be increased.

3. The third issue that I want to raise relates to the relationship between hours of work and production. I fear that if hours were cut to 35 hours a week the reduction in output on the part of the presently employed workers would be greater than the increase in output due to the hiring of more workers. Thinking in terms of the former group, it must be said that the relationship between hours and output is a matter on which there is very little satisfactory information.

This particular problem is raised ordinarily during times of great national emergency, and during the period of World War I and again during World War II some careful thought was given to the relationship between hours and output, but at other times very little attention has been given to this highly important issue.

Perhaps the chief reason is that it is extremely difficult to figure out this relationship and I believe, moreover, that a good many employers are not willing to experiment in their own plants in the matter of varying hours and studying the output consequences. As a consequence we must rely, at the present time at least, largely on general reasoning. But that doesn't mean, however, that our conclusions are therefore invalid.

At the time of the great campaign for the 8-hour day back in the 1890s, and it was carried on both in England and in this country, two English authors, Sidney Webb and Harold Cox, declared that, "Experience shows that, in the arithmetic of labor . . . 2 from 10 is likely to produce, not 8 but even 11." Strange things may well happen in the arithmetic of labor, and it is quite possible that at that time there were industries and employments in which more could have been produced, at least ultimately, in an 8-hour day than in a 10-hour day. And this is what Webb and Cox were hinting at in their rather paradoxical statement.

A reduction in hours can lead to less absenteeism and fewer accidents. Studies made during World War II tend to confirm these results. A reduction in hours may also lead to a faster pace of work. But if the cut in hours is at all considerable the influence of these factors may not be great enough to offset the production effect of fewer hours on the job.

Moreover, there is an inconsistency between the greater production argument for shorter hours and the unemployment argument. The latter argument, at least in its simple form, is really based on the assumption that there is just so much work to be done, that there is what economists sometimes call a fixed work fund.

If this is the case, it follows that to give every worker a job, the length of the workweek enjoyed by the present workers must be reduced. However, and here is the inconsistency, if now we argue that shorter hours will increase production not only per hour, but per week, then it follows that there will be even fewer employment opportunities and thus the volume of unemployment will increase.

If one could be sure that in consequence of reducing the workweek from 40 to 35 hours, as many new workers would be employed as to make possible the complete utilization of the released hours, it is possible that production would not suffer. Conceivably it might increase. But for reasons given previously, under point 2, it is not likely that production would be maintained, let alone increased.

4. My fourth point relates to our living standards and is inseparably connected with the general question just discussed. It is an economic truism that the material living standards of a nation are basically determined by its per-capita output. It is also a fact that despite all the talk to the contrary, there are mil-

lions of Americans who are either living in poverty or in a condition of deprivation. For millions of our fellow citizens we certainly have not achieved the era of affluence.

It would seem, then, that any policy which would pull down our production or slow up its growth rate still more is undesirable. At the present time, and looking at the matter in terms of average living standards, perhaps we can afford to alter the work-leisure ratio to some degree. But certainly not by very much.

In short, the 35-hour workweek is a luxury which we cannot yet afford. To be sure, we will achieve it in the future, just as we will attain the 30-hour week. Indeed, in time we will reach the standard that Harry Van Arsdale and his Electrical Workers in New York already have.[1] I might say parenthetically that it would be a national economic calamity if this standard were forced upon all employers at the present time. The point that I would like to emphasize is that there is a danger that we may reduce hours too fast; that is, in terms of the long-run permanent effects on living standards.

5. This leads us to a consideration of hours of work in relation to the international situation. In view of this situation, including the existence of a "production battle" with Soviet Russia and certainly Mr. Khrushchev has made it plain that Russia is engaged in such a battle with us, it would seem ill advised for us to adopt a policy that would unduly slow up, if not decrease, our growth rate.

It is rather disconcerting that at a time when Soviet Russia is trying to pull 5 or 6 million more women into its work force, and it has been engaged in this in the last two or three years and expects to achieve that goal by 1965, it is rather disconcerting under those conditions to find ourselves seriously thinking about the necessity of cutting hours—or encouraging early retirement—as a means of providing jobs.

It is disturbing to think that while Russia is pressing vigorously to increase production—with about 75 percent of her workers on piece-work, which is much higher than the percentage in this country—we are considering a policy that could curtail production.

1. Electrical workers in New York City have a contract specifying a basic 25-hour workweek and 5 hours overtime at time and one half.

Advocacy of a permanent reduction in hours as a means for spreading work is indeed a counsel of desperation. Under the circumstances that have existed for the past few years, with our high unemployment rates, such advocacy is easily understandable, however.

I might say that I do not blame the unions for emphasizing the necessity of reducing hours, although I think that such a policy would not achieve the effects anticipated, and, in ways that I am pointing to at the present time, would be undesirable.

With reference to the underdeveloped nations of the world it might be added that they are likely to be more favorably impressed, and more extensively aided in one way or another, by an increase in our output than an increase in our leisure. They might envy us with an increase in our leisure, but I am not certain that they would respect us.

6. My sixth point: Nothing has been said so far about the money costs of shorter hours. This is highly important. If hours were to be reduced to 35 hours a week, and take-home pay were to remain the same, hourly wage costs for the present workers would increase by 14.3 percent. I might add if the cut were to 36 hours the increase would be 11.1 percent. If it were cut to 37 hours, it would be 8.1 percent.

Presumably the new workers who would be taken on, and who in most instances would be less well qualified than those currently employed, would receive the same increased rates.

Such a wage increase would be exceedingly burdensome to many employers and probably force some into bankruptcy. To some degree the increased wage cost might be passed on to the consumers—which would be small comfort to them. Or it might in part come out of profits. This, however, would tend to diminish investments on the part of domestic investors, and further discourage foreign investments in the country which have already dropped very steeply.

From the preceding presentation it is clear that I do not favor a permanent reduction in hours, at the same take-home pay, as a means for dealing with the unemployment caused by technological and other structural changes in our economy. The problem before us must be approached, and should be approached, in other ways—ways that I shall not here attempt to discuss since this raises the whole large issue of the manifold policies for coping with technological and other structural unemployment. My concern at the present is with the matter of reducing hours.

As far as hours are concerned, however, there is a further point I would like to make. In my presentation I have spoken a number of times about a permanent reduction in hours and once or twice alluded to a temporary reduction. These must be distinguished. Over the years the latter policy, with hourly wages but not daily wages remaining the same, has often been used for coping with seasonal and cyclical unemployment.

I believe it would be advantageous to use it on a more extensive scale to deal with the current unemployment situation.

A temporary sharing of work and sharing of wages has much to commend it, and I would like to see both unions and employers pressing more vigorously for its adoption. Such a policy does not mean that the workers should be denied their "normal" wage increases—approximately equal each year to the annual increase in man-hour productivity in the economy as a whole. It does mean, however, that the unions would not press for an additional wage increase through the use of the same-take-home-pay principle.

Under our type of economic system the economic health of the country is tied up with profit prospects. If these prospects are greatly darkened by extreme hour demands, or extreme wage demands, the growth rate of the economy is likely to suffer.

There is the other side of the coin, to be sure. Adequate effective demand—sufficient monetary purchasing power—is of great importance. But if such demand in the economy as a whole is not large enough, it seems to me it would be best to stimulate its expansion by monetary and fiscal policies rather than by exerting pressure on individual employers through such means as decreasing hours and maintaining take-home pay. I might say I am speaking here of sizable reductions in hours. . . .

Can a Case Be Made for Discouraging Overtime?

T. ALDRICH FINEGAN

T. Aldrich Finegan is assistant professor of economics at Vanderbilt University. This essay, commenting critically on President Johnson's proposal to increase the overtime rate, first appeared in Challenge *in April 1964.*

THE FAIR LABOR STANDARDS ACT of 1938 provides that most production workers in manufacturing and many nonprofessional and nonsupervisory workers in other industries must be paid at least one and one-half times their regular hourly earnings for each hour of work over 40 per week in a single establishment. For a number of years organized labor has been urging the reduction of the regular workweek to 35 in order to provide more jobs for the unemployed. Notwithstanding the growing concern over unemployment, this proposal has encountered a frosty reception, not only from the Eisenhower, Kennedy, and Johnson administrations, but from the overwhelming majority of economists as well. Thus prospects for a reduction in the standard workweek remain dim.

In the past few months, increased attention has been given to another facet of the Fair Labor Standards Act—the minimum rate at which covered workers must be compensated for overtime. It has been proposed that the rate be increased from time and a half to double time—at least in some covered industries. The theory is that if overtime work were made more costly, employers would rely on it less and instead would hire more workers, thus reducing unemployment.

Unlike the shorter workweek proposal, the higher premium for overtime will receive serious Congressional consideration and may be enacted into law. In his economic report to Congress on January 20, 1964, President Johnson stated that "the regular use of heavy overtime may be unreasonably curtailing job opportunities in some industries." He added that he would request legislation "authorizing higher overtime penalty rates on an industry-by-industry basis where tripartite industry committees determine that such rates could create more jobs without unduly raising costs." Ten days later the President submitted his proposal to Congress.

While I shall argue that the overtime rate should not be increased at this time, either generally or in selected industries, it is only fair that I begin by conceding (1) the seriousness of the unemployment problem, (2) the erosion of the present penalty rate as a deterrent to overtime work, and (3) the likelihood that a higher premium would reduce unemployment somewhat.

In recent years our unemployment rate has hovered between 5½ and 6 percent of the civilian labor force. This rate of joblessness may not seem high when compared with the "target" rate of four percent—the lowest rate many economists feel is consistent with changing patterns of technology and demand, normal labor mobility and a reasonable degree of price stability.

But the appearance is deceptive. The present unemployment rate is only one manifestation of the persistent underutilization of our human and material resources. In addition to the four million unemployed, over two million part-time workers want full-time work but cannot find it. Furthermore, many individuals (no one yet knows just how many) have become so discouraged in seeking jobs that they have temporarily withdrawn from the labor force (as we presently measure it). There are also some workers who have lost skilled jobs and have been compelled to accept unskilled employment as a stop-gap.

Thus the aggregate underutilization of our human resources is much greater than the gap between the target and actual unemployment rates would suggest. The Council of Economic Advisers has estimated that the slack in our economy during 1963 cost us roughly $30 billion of foregone GNP.

There is also some evidence that the statutory overtime premium (time and a half) is less of a deterrent to overtime work at present than it was a decade ago. To be sure, the amount of overtime is still quite responsive to short-run fluctuations in the business cycle, rising during periods of business expansion and declining during recessions. But it has not been reduced by the persistence of abnormally high unemployment during the past several years.

In manufacturing, for example, the number of employed production workers fell from 13.4 million in 1956 to 12.4 million in 1962, while the number of unemployed increased sharply. Yet the average weekly amount of overtime per worker was the same (2.8 hours) in 1962 as it was in 1956. According to the Bureau of Labor Statistics, manufacturing production workers in 1962 put in 34.7 million hours of overtime per week at a payroll cost of $120.4 million, including some $40 million in premium pay. The Bureau also estimates that "overtime hours accounted for 6.9 percent of total paid man-hours in manufacturing and 10.1 percent of total payroll" during that year.

Overtime has become less of a deterrent because of the steadily growing cost of fringe benefits. Benefits such as pensions, insurance and paid vacations depend more on the size and turnover of the work force than on the length of the workweek, and they are not part of the regular hourly wage on which overtime is computed. Thus the 50 percent premium on straight-time hourly wages may, in many cases, turn out to be only a 40 percent increase in hourly labor costs.

Nevertheless, *some* of the overtime work undertaken at a premium of time and a half would not be undertaken if double time had to be paid. A higher penalty rate, at least up to some point, would also encourage employers to substitute straight-time labor for overtime labor—that is, to hire more workers. Furthermore, the combination of greater employment and less overtime would lead to a more equitable distribution of employment opportunities, an objective which in itself is desirable.

Clearly, then, the proposal does have some merit. What are its disadvantages?

First, an increase in the overtime premium would tend to *reduce* both our total utilization of labor and our aggregate output of goods and services. True, the number of persons employed would rise and the number unemployed would fall. But what would happen to the aggregate number of man-hours worked? The latter would surely decline. The reason is quite simple. There are some overtime jobs—especially those of short duration—for which it is not economical to hire additional workers. If overtime labor costs increase, fewer of these jobs will be undertaken. As a result, the decline in overtime hours would probably exceed the added hours of regular work.

If the impact on aggregate man-hours of employment is adverse, real output, at least over the short run, will decline—provided other things, including aggregate demand, remain unchanged. Of course, other factors may vary so as to prevent a fall in aggregate output. For example, the substitution of straight-time work for overtime might be accompanied by a rise in the average level of worker efficiency. Also, if the reduction in overtime work were quite small, the aggregate wage bill would rise, making possible some increase in aggregate demand. But under these circumstances there would be little point in raising the overtime premium, since the increase in employment would also be small.

Thus, while a higher overtime premium would bring about some reduction in the rate of unemployment, it would probably *increase* our underutilization of labor (measured in man-hours) and the gap between our actual and potential GNP (measured in constant dollars). It would reduce the appearance but not the substance of economic slack and would impair the usefulness of the unemployment rate as a measure of that slack. It would, in short, simply spread less work more evenly.

The second problem concerns the impact of a higher overtime rate on consumer prices and the ability of some firms to increase output in response to an unexpected increase in demand. The intent of the President's plan is to raise the overtime rate only in industries where the employment effect would be large and the cost effect small. But how many industries would pass this test, and how successful would the tripartite industry boards (representing management, labor and the public) be in identifying them?

It is easy, of course, to exaggerate the inflationary potential of higher labor costs, particularly under a policy of monetary restraint; overtime payments, after all, are only a small fraction of total payroll costs. There is no point, however, in pretending that the potential is nil. Surely higher overtime costs will eventually be reflected in higher prices of those goods and services that use overtime labor in their production.

What is worse, most of the inflationary pressures of a higher overtime rate would not become apparent until the present gap between actual and potential GNP is reduced and the economy approaches full employment. The immediate effect of a higher premium might be a substantial cutback in overtime work. But as we reduce economic slack, both the use of overtime and its impact on costs will increase.

Furthermore, the higher the cost of overtime, the greater will be the tendency of firms operating at normal production levels to respond to increased demand by raising prices instead of increasing output through overtime work. Thus, not only would the proposal increase inflationary pressures associated with a movement toward full employment, it would also reduce the upward "output flexibility" of establishments subject to the higher penalty rate.

Some increase in costs and prices is, of course, to be expected as the labor market becomes tighter. But this fact hardly justifies legislation that will aggravate the problem.

The third disadvantage of higher overtime rates, even if established on an industry-by-industry basis, would be their uneven impact on the labor costs of various firms. In many cases, this differential impact would be hard to justify on grounds of equity or efficiency. After all, employers resort to overtime for many reasons besides the desire to economize on fringe benefits. A good deal of overtime work is the result of emergency situations: machinery sometimes breaks down; bottlenecks in production occur; some workers fail to report for work. Also, some firms have more limited facilities than others; some have greater shortages of workers with critical skills; some are less certain about the strength of future demand. The application of a high penalty rate on all kinds of overtime would thus be illogical. On the other hand, any attempt to apply different rates to each type of overtime work would surely encounter imposing obstacles.

The fourth and final drawback is that a higher overtime premium would probably increase the problem of "rationing" overtime work among production workers eager to earn overtime pay. Everyone will agree that workers putting in overtime hours should be fully compensated. Assuming that overtime legislation is needed to insure that production workers are, in fact, adequately compensated for overtime, is there any evidence that the present minimum compensation of time and a half is generally inadequate?

This important question merits careful study. One can surely find instances in which workers have been forced rather than induced into doing overtime work. But this appears to be the exception rather than the rule. Numerous union officials have testified that most grievances on this subject arise not because workers have been made to work overtime, but because they have been deprived of a chance to do so. Unless this information is very inaccurate, the present premium is more than adequate to cover the psychic costs of most overtime work. Indeed, the fact that some three million workers hold down two or more jobs suggests that a good many persons might be willing to work overtime without any premium.

To put this point in more traditional economic terms, it would appear that in most unionized establishments the minimum rate for overtime set by the Fair Labor Standards Act is somewhat higher than the price that would "clear the market" for overtime work. If so, an increase in the statutory premium would make it even more difficult to achieve an equitable allocation of overtime.

The essential weakness of the President's proposal is its failure to deal with the real causes of high unemployment—structural maladjustments and inadequate aggregate demand. Instead, it seeks to *redistribute* aggregate man-hours of work among a larger number of workers. While this redistribution may appeal to our sense of justice, the device by which it would be achieved has several undesirable side effects—not the least of which is a reduction in the amount of work that, at given levels of demand, would be available for redistribution. . . .

We should do some hard thinking about what role, if any, overtime legislation should play in our economy. The hours provision of the Fair Labor Standards Act, however, was clearly not the product of any such analysis. A study of the Congressional hearings and debates that preceded the passage of the act indicates that the overtime clause was primarily intended to serve as a work-spreading mechanism—a means of redistributing employment opportunities in the midst of a prolonged and severe depression. This goal may have been appropriate in the 1930s, but is it appropriate today?

What contribution does the overtime law make to the solution of our major economic challenges of this decade—the underutilization of our human and nonhuman resources, the chronic poverty of families in depressed areas, our balance of payments difficulties, the manifold problems of automation, and a slow but persistent rise in consumer prices? Obviously no single law can solve all our problems, but does the present overtime proposal serve any constructive purpose at all?

The reasons economists have traditionally advanced in support of legislative limitations on hours of work no longer seem compelling. In how many industries, for example, is federal legislation still needed to prevent an excessively long workweek which would endanger the health of blue-collar workers and would diminish their efficiency? And even if a few such industries could be found, would they justify legislative restraints as far-reaching and indiscriminate as those provided by the Fair Labor Standards Act? If we do not need sweeping overtime legislation to prevent a workweek injurious to health or efficiency or to cope intelligently with the problem of unemployment, why *do* we need it?

True, it is still possible that in the absence of federal legislation certain employers might exploit workers through overtime work. Were it not for the act, some employers might pay smaller overtime premiums or require more overtime work than would prevail under effective competition among employers for the services of workers. But the protection that unions presently provide against such exploitation is very widespread. In fact, it extends not only to union members but also to most other workers who could join unions of they wished.

Moreover, in those relatively few cases in which workers are not protected by either unions or effective competition for labor, the overtime clause is likely to be of little value in preventing labor exploitation. This is because the law does not prescribe the "regular rate of pay" on which overtime must be calculated, save that this rate must not fall short of the minimum established by the wage provisions of the act (currently $1.25 for most workers). Except for this restriction, there is nothing in the act to prevent an employer from paying his workers substantially lower wages *for both regular and overtime work* than they could earn in more competitive labor markets. In short, the protection offered by the overtime clause to unorganized workers in noncompetitive labor markets will be largely inadequate; to those in competitive markets it will be largely unnecessary.

Finally, would hours of work in manufacturing and other covered industries substantially increase in the absence of statutory restraints? The answer, in my judgment, is no. Somewhat more overtime would be worked, but the scheduled or normal workweek in most establishments would not be lengthened. The reason is twofold. First, the 40-hour week is so firmly entrenched in both custom and most union contracts as the norm for blue-collar workers that a return to a longer workweek is very unlikely—barring a national emergency. When a change in this norm occurs, it will be downward, not upward.

Second, the basic reason for the secular decline in hours of work has been the long-run rise in real hourly earnings. While the Fair Labor Standards Act may have brought the 40 hour week to covered industries *sooner* than otherwise, virtually all of them would have adopted it by now. At least that is what a projection of the trend in hours prior to 1929 suggests.

I do not contend that within the context of our economy a persuasive case for federal overtime legislation *cannot* be made. I merely say that it *has not* been made. The issue deserves to be settled by investigation and discussion, not by default.

Suggested Further Readings

AFL-CIO, *Camouflage: The Myth of "Labor Monopoly"* (Industrial Union Department, Washington, D.C., 1960).

Bowen, W. G., *The Wage Price Issue: A Theoretical Analysis* (Princeton, 1960).

———, *Wage Behavior in the Postwar Period: An Empirical Analysis* (Princeton, Industrial Relations Section, 1961).

Bradley, Philip, ed., *The Public Stake in Union Power* (University of Virginia Press, 1959).

Chamberlin, Edward H., *The Economic Analysis of Labor Union Power* (American Enterprise Institute, 1963).

Denison, Edward F., "Hours of Work," Chs. 5–6 in *The Sources of Economic Growth in the United States* (Committee for Economic Development, 1962).

Eckstein, Otto, and Wilson T., "The Determination of Money Wages in American Industry," *Quarterly Journal of Economics*, August 1962.

Fellner, W., *et al.*, *The Problem of Rising Prices* (OECD, 1961).

Greenbaum, Marcia L., *The Shorter Workweek*, New York State School of Industrial and Labor Relations Bulletin 50, June 1963.

Gordon, R. A., "Has Structural Unemployment Worsened?", *Industrial Relations*, May 1964.

Kravis, I. B., "Relative Income Shares in Fact and Theory," *American Economic Review*, December 1959.

Leiserson, Mark, "A Brief Interpretative Survey of Wage-Price Problems in Western Europe," Study Paper No. 11, Joint Economic Committee, *Study of Employment, Growth, and Price Levels*, December 1959.

Lester, R. A., "Reflections on the 'Labor Monopoly' Issue," *Journal of Political Economy*, December 1947.

Levinson, Harold, *Unionism, Wage Trends, and Income Distribution, 1914–1947*, Michigan Business Studies, Vol. X, No. 4, 1951.

———, "Postwar Movements of Prices and Wages in Manufacturing Industries," Study Paper No. 21, Joint Economic Committee, *Study of Employment, Growth, and Price Levels*, January 1960.

Lewis, Gregg, *Unionism and Relative Wages in the United States* (University of Chicago, 1963).

Machlup, Fritz, "Another View of Cost-push and Demand-pull Inflation," *Review of Economics and Statistics*, May 1960.

Mason, Edward S., "Labor Monopoly and All That," Industrial Relations Research Association, *Proceedings of the Eighth Annual Meeting* (1955).

Peterson, John, "Employment Effects of Minimum Wages, 1938–1950", *Journal of Political Economy*, October 1957.

———, "Employment Effects of State Minimum Wages for Women: Three Historical Cases Reexamined," *Industrial and Labor Relations Review*,

April 1959, and "Comment" by Lester and "Reply" by Peterson in same journal, January 1960.

Phillips, A. W., "The Relation Between Unemployment and the Rate of Change of Money Wage Rates in the United Kingdom, 1861–1957," *Economica*, November 1958.

Reder, Melvin W., "Alternative Theories of Labor's Share," in *The Allocation of Economic Resources* (Stanford, 1959).

———, "Wage Structure Theory and Measurement," in *Aspects of Labor Economics* (National Bureau of Economic Research, 1962).

Rees, Albert, *The Economics of Trade Unions* (University of Chicago Press, 1962).

Reynolds, Lloyd, *The Structure of Labor Markets* (Harper & Row, 1951).

Rottenberg, Simon, "On Choice in Labor Markets," *Industrial and Labor Relations Review*, January 1956, and "Comments" by Lampman and Lester and "Reply" by Rottenberg in same journal, July 1956.

Wright, David McCord, ed., *The Impact of the Union* (Harcourt, Brace & World, 1961).